Building Spelling Skills

Written and Designed by Garry J. Moes

Editors:
Dr. Paul D. Lindstrom
Michael J. McHugh

Book 4

CHRISTIAN LIBERTY PRESS

A PUBLICATION OF
Christian Liberty Press

© Copyright 1992
Christian Liberty Press
502 W. Euclid Avenue
Arlington Heights, Illinois 60004
USA

TABLE OF CONTENTS

PREFACE

Dear Teacher or Parent:

In a day and age when standards and rules are often considered obstacles to creativity and freedom of expression, a reliance on rules in academic pursuits may be viewed by some as outmoded and destructive.

Spelling the words of the English language, however, if taken seriously, must take account of standard rules. At the same time, it is recognized that American English has had a wide variety of influences and thus is difficult to force into consistent molds. The author and editors believe it is helpful for students to comprehend the basic rules of spelling, and therefore this book provides a Spelling Guide for each unit. Students who have learned a few simple rules will be able to understand how to correctly spell thousands of words. For these words, as well as the many exceptions, the practice of repeated writing of spelling words will imprint precise spelling into the mind of the student.

Instructors are encouraged to keep reading and spelling in close fellowship with each other during the teaching process. It is also helpful to keep in mind that there are no shortcuts on the road to developing good spellers. Good spellers are developed by a teacher's hard work, persistence and encouragement, not to mention the same for the student.

TEACHING SUGGESTIONS

In addition to the instructions given for each unit and lesson, the following approaches are offered by way of suggestion to help teachers better guide their students to good spelling:

1. Read all of the words from the Unit Word List aloud with your student.

2. Emphasize to the student the primary spelling rule contained in the lesson. Explain the rule and provide examples.

3. Quiz the student by asking him to spell each of the words from the lesson on separate paper as you read each of them aloud.

4. Check the accuracy of the student's written work and help the student understand why he misspelled certain words.

5. Have your student provide the correct spelling for any words he misspelled on separate paper or on a chalkboard.

6. Show the student how some of the words from the unit are used in a sentence. This exercise will help to improve the student's comprehension, pronunciation skills, and vocabulary. Students should be encouraged to use some of their spelling words in sentences of their own choosing.

7. Conclude each unit with a review of that unit's words and a final test. Finally, you may wish to review words from the current unit or previous ones before starting into a new unit or exercise.

May the Lord bless you with success as you train students for His glory!

CURSIVE ALPHABET

Aa Bb Cc Dd Ee

Ff Gg Hh Ii Jj

Kk Ll Mm Nn

Oo Pp Qq Rr Ss

Tt Uu Vv Ww

Xx Yy Zz

LEARNING HOW TO SPELL WORDS

1. Look at the word. Study every letter.

2. Say the word to yourself.

3. Say it again aloud, and then spell it.

4. Copy the word on paper, naming the letters as you write.

5. Close your spelling book, and test yourself.
   Write the word.
   Do not worry if you do not get it right the first time.

6. Open your spelling book again. Check the word.

7. Study the word one more time, and test yourself
   by writing the word again.

* * * * *

As with all of your school work, always remember to ask God to help you learn and understand what you are doing. Thank Him for His help with every lesson.

WORD ENDINGS

LESSON 1 - Vocabulary

Election Time

Circle the list words in these sentences. Spell the list words aloud. Write the sentences on a separate sheet of paper.

1. Our nation chooses its leaders by a vote of the people, which is called an election.

2. Citizens vote using a secret ballot.

3. In a democracy, the majority rules.

4. When a candidate wins more votes than all other candidates, he has a plurality.

5. A political campaign may include rallies, speeches, and a debate.

6. A pollster is someone who tries to find out how people will be voting.

7. Each party holds a meeting, or convention.

WORD LIST

nation
motion
donation
mention
subtraction
multiplication
addition
convention
vacation
election
candidate
political
ballot
campaign
pollster
voting
debate
plurality
majority
conversation

LESSON 2 - Practice

1. Study the word list for Unit 1. Understand the meaning of each word.
2. Write each word twice on a separate paper.

LESSON 3 - Spelling Guide

> The suffixes '-tion' and '-ion' may be added to base words to create a noun form. The base word must often be changed before adding the suffix.

1. Make list words out of the following base words and suffixes '-tion' or '-ion.'

multiply + ca + tion

_____

donate + ion

_____

subtract + ion

_____

add + i + tion

_____

vacate + ion

_____

elect + ion

_____

convene + tion

_____

move + tion

_____

2. Thinking about spelling.

    a. How did you change 'multiply' before adding the suffix?

    b. How did you change 'donate,' 'vacate,' 'converse,' and 'convene' before adding the suffix?

    c. How did you change 'move' before adding the suffix?

3. Write all the words in your word list one more time on a separate paper.

LESSON 4 - Exercise

1. Study the ten words from your Unit 1 list printed at the right. Write the correct words to fit the following clues.

a. A way of choosing people to be leaders

_____

> *Choose one of these words for this exercise:*
>
> election
>
> political
>
> candidate
>
> ballot
>
> campaign
>
> pollster
>
> voting
>
> debate
>
> majority
>
> plurality

b. A person seeking office, a contestant

_____

c. A card or paper on which to mark choices in an election

_____

d. Having to do with politics

_____

e. Someone who tries to find out people's opinions

_____

f. An effort to become elected, a crusade

_____

g. A discussion of different ideas

_____

h. Making choices in an election

_____

i. More than one-half of the votes   j. More votes than any others

_____   _____

2. Take your first practice test on all words in the Unit 1 word list.

LESSON 5

Review your word list and take your final test. Write the words in the spaces provided at the back of this book. Pray for God's help before you take the test.

UNIT 2

WORD ENDINGS

LESSON 1 - Vocabulary

The Great Outdoors

Circle the list words in these sentences. Spell the list words aloud. Write the sentences on a separate sheet of paper.

1. We like to go camping and fishing on our family vacation.

2. We often go boating and swimming at the lake.

3. Jim skipped a stone across the pond.

4. In the autumn, I go hunting with my uncle.

5. Running and jogging are good outdoor exercises.

6. Bob climbed a mountain at Yosemite National Park.

7. Mom and Dad walked along the seashore at sunset.

WORD LIST

shipped
wrapped
slipped
plotted
grabbed
planting
dusting
filming
cracking
spanking
camping
walked
jogging
hunting
climbed
swimming
running
fishing
skipped
boating

LESSON 2 - Practice

1. Study the word list for Unit 2. Understand the meaning of each word.
2. Write each word twice on a separate paper.

LESSON 3 - Spelling Guide

> When a word ends with a short vowel plus a consonant, the last consonant is doubled before adding a suffix that begins with a vowel.
>
> When a word ends with two consonants, the last consonant is NOT doubled before adding a suffix that begins with a vowel.

1. Form list words with the following words and suffixes. Using the Spelling Guide above, decide whether or not to double the last consonant before adding the suffix.

a. ship + ed	f. hunt + ing	k. fish + ing
_____	_____	_____
b. plot + ed	g. swim + ing	l. skip + ed
_____	_____	_____
c. plant + ing	h. boat + ing	m. grab + ed
_____	_____	_____
d. crack + ing	i. spank + ing	n. wrap + ed
_____	_____	_____
e. jog + ing	j. walk + ed	o. film + ing
_____	_____	_____

2. Write all the words in your word list one more time on a separate paper.

LESSON 4 - Exercise

1. Write the words below three times, adding the suffix in the box. Remember to double the last consonant in the base word when the rule requires doubling.

	-ed	-ing	-er
slip	_____	_____	_____
dust	_____	_____	_____
camp	_____	_____	_____
climb	_____	_____	_____
run	xxxxxxxxxx	_____	_____

2. Thinking about spelling.
   a. Did you double the 'p' in slip before adding the suffixes? Why or why not?
   b. Did you double the 't' in dust before adding the suffixes? Why or why not?
   c. Did you double the 'p' in camp before adding the suffixes? Why or why not?
   d. Did you double the 'b' in climb before adding the suffixes? Why or why not?
   e. Did you double the 'n' in run before adding the suffixes? Why or why not?
   f. Notice the X's in the '-ed' column after run. That's because there is no such word as 'runned.' (Do you know the proper past form of run?)

3. Take your first practice test on all words in the Unit 2 word list.

LESSON 5

Review your word list and take your final test. Write the words in the spaces provided at the back of this book. Be sure to ask for God's help with your test.

UNIT 3

WORD ENDINGS

LESSON 1 - Vocabulary

Christian Attitudes

Circle the list words in these sentences. Spell the list words aloud. Write the sentences on a separate sheet of paper.

1. A loving heart is one that is serving God and others.

2. We should try to give encouragement to those who are discouraged.

3. The Holy Spirit is our Helper as we are striving for improvement in our attitudes.

4. Hating and being hateful are ungodly attitudes.

5. God asks us to surrender our thoughts and hearts to Him entirely and completely.

6. Each Christian is called to be a partaker in Christ's holiness.

7. "Whatsoever things are lovely ... think on these things" (Philippians 4:8).

WORD LIST

surprised
promised
improvement
lively
lovely
hiking
liked
provided
basement
safely
loving
service
encouragement
hating
hateful
striving
completely
entirely
partaker
saving

14

LESSON 2 - Practice

1. Study the word list for Unit 3. Understand the meaning of each word.
2. Write each word twice on a separate paper.

LESSON 3 - Spelling Guide

> Drop final 'e' from base words before adding a suffix beginning with a vowel.
> Keep final 'e' on base words when adding a suffix beginning with a consonant.

1. Form list words with the following base words and suffixes. Using the Spelling Guide above, decide whether to drop or keep the final 'e' before adding the suffix.

a. save + ing   f. serve + ing   k. love + ly

_____   _____   _____

b. entire + ly   g. base + ment   l. love + ing

_____   _____   _____

c. partake + er   h. provide + ed   m. promise + ed

_____   _____   _____

d. hate + ing   i. hike + ing   n. improve + ment

_____   _____   _____

e. hate + ful   j. like + ed   o. encourage + ment

_____   _____   _____

2. Write all the words in your word list one more time on a separate paper.

1. Write all the list words with the suffixes indicated in the boxes at the left.

| -er |
| -ful |
| -ment |
| -ed |

| -ly |
| -ing |

2. Thinking about spelling.
   a. Why do 'base,' 'improve' and 'encourage' keep final 'e' before the suffix '-ment' is added?
   b. Why do 'surprise,' 'promise,' 'like' and 'provide' drop final 'e' before the suffix '-ed' is added?

3. Take your first practice test on all words in the Unit 3 word list.

LESSON 5

Review your word list and take your final test. Write the words in the spaces provided at the back of this book. Be sure to ask for God's help with your test.

UNIT 4

WORD ENDINGS

LESSON 1 - Vocabulary

God's Loving Care

Circle the list words in these Bible verses. Spell the list words aloud. Write the verses on a separate sheet of paper.

1. "I tell you, do not worry about your life" (Matthew 6:25, NIV).

2. "Therefore we are buried with him by baptism..., even so we also should walk in newness of life" (Romans 6:4).

3. "In his love and in his pity, he redeemed them" (Isaiah 63:9).

4. "The children of Judah prevailed, because they relied upon the Lord God of their fathers" (2 Chronicles 13:18).

5. "If we believe not, yet he abideth faithful: he cannot deny himself" (2 Timothy 2:13).

6. "But my God shall supply all your need according to his riches in glory by Christ Jesus" (Philippians 4:19).

7. "Knowing this, that the trying of your faith worketh patience" (James 1:3).

WORD LIST

worry
worried
worrying
bury
buried
burying
pity
pitied
pitying
rely
relied
relying
deny
denied
denying
supply
supplied
supplying
try
tried
trying

LESSON 2 - Practice

1. Study the word list for Unit 4. Understand the meaning of each word.
2. Write each word twice on a separate paper.

LESSON 3 - Spelling Guide

> When a word ends in a consonant plus 'y,' the 'y' is changed to 'i' before adding the suffixes '-ed,' '-er' or '-es.'
> When a word ends in a consonant plus 'y,' the 'y' is NOT changed before adding the suffix '-ing.'

1. Add the suffixes '-es,' '-er,' '-ed' and '-ing' to these list words. Using the Spelling Guide above, decide whether or not to change the 'y' to 'i' before adding the suffixes.

worry

bury

pity

_____

_____

_____

_____

_____

_____

_____

_____

_____

_____

_____

_____

rely

deny

supply

_____

_____

_____

_____

_____

_____

_____

_____

_____

_____

_____

_____

2. Thinking about spelling.

try

a. Which suffixes require you to change 'y' to 'i'?

_____

_____

b. Which suffix does not require you to change 'y' to 'i'?

_____

_____

3. Write all the words in your word list one more time on a separate paper.

1. Write the correct form of these list words in the blanks in the sentences below. Choose one of the following forms:

   * the base word at the left
   * the form ending with '-ed'
   * the form ending with '-ing'

pity	→ a. Take _____ on the poor.
rely	→ b. Your parents are _____ on you to pass your test.
try	→ c. Tammy _____ to call you on the phone yesterday.
worry	→ d. Do not _____ about tomorrow.
bury	→ e. The soldiers _____ the dead when the battle ended.
supply	→ f. Mom and Dad are _____ food for the party.
deny	→ g. Peter _____ Jesus three times after His arrest.

2. 'Worried' is the past form (past tense) of 'worry.' Write all of the other list words that are in the past tense.

   _____   _____   _____

   _____   _____   _____

3. Take your first practice test on all words in the Unit 4 word list.

LESSON 5

Review your word list and take your final test. Write the words in the spaces provided at the back of this book. Remember to ask for God's help.

UNIT 5

PLURAL WORD ENDINGS

LESSON 1 - Vocabulary

Business and Industry

Circle the list words in these sentences. Spell the list words aloud. Write the sentences on a separate sheet of paper.

1. Businesses involving many people are sometimes called companies.

2. Manufacturing and trading companies may be called industries.

3. Some industries have factories where products are made.

4. Businesses that make bread are bakeries.

5. Factories where food is preserved in cans are called canneries.

6. Trucks make deliveries of goods to and from businesses and factories.

7. Batteries are made in factories.

WORD LIST

companies
industries
bakeries
deliveries
factories
batteries
canneries
canaries
enemies
treaties
spies
countries
counties
allies
alleys
monkeys
donkeys
chimneys
journeys
guys

LESSON 2 - Practice

1. Study the word list for Unit 5. Understand the meaning of each word.
2. Write each word twice on a separate paper.

LESSON 3 - Spelling Guide

> The plural of nouns ending with a consonant plus 'y' is made by changing the 'y' to 'i' and adding 'es.'
>
> The plural of nouns ending with a vowal plus 'y" is made by simply adding 's.'

1. Write the plurals of these nouns. Using the Spelling Guide above, decide whether or not to change the 'y' to 'i' before adding the plural ending.

a. battery_____

b. cannery_____

c. canary_____

d. enemy_____

e. treaty_____

f. monkey_____

g. company_____

h. donkey_____

i. bakery_____

h. chimney_____

k. delivery_____

l. journey_____

m. guy_____

n. factory_____

o. spy_____

p. ally_____

q. alley_____

r. country_____

s. county_____

t. industry_____

2. Thinking about spelling.

a. Did you change the 'y" to 'i" to make the plural of 'monkey'? Why or why not?

b. Did you change the 'y" to 'i" to make the plural of 'enemy'? Why or why not?

c. Did you change the 'y" to 'i" to make the plural of 'guy'? Why or why not?

d. Did you change the 'y" to 'i" to make the plural of 'journey'? Why or why not?

e. Did you change the 'y" to 'i" to make the plural of 'county'? Why or why not?

f. Did you change the 'y" to 'i" to make the plural of 'donkey'? Why or why not?

3. Write all the words in your word list one more time on a separate paper.

1. The Unit 5 word list has four sets of words in which the words are similar, but have slightly different spellings and completely different meanings. Write the words and carefully notice the differences in spelling. Provide the singular form of each word that you write in the spaces below.

cannery

canneries - factories where food is preserved in cans.

_____

canary

canaries - small songbirds that make good house pets.

_____

_____
_____
[**countries** - nations; lands where people are citizens.
  counties - small divisions of a state or province.

_____
_____
[**allies** - people or nations joined in a common purpose.
  alleys - narrow streets or bowling lanes.

_____
_____
[**monkeys** - small, long-tailed animals that swing in trees.
  donkeys - long-eared animals similar to small horses.

2. Take your first practice test on all words in the Unit 5 word list.

LESSON 5

Review your word list and take your final test. Write the words in the spaces provided at the back of this book. Remember to ask God for His help.

UNIT 6

PLURAL WORD ENDINGS

LESSON 1 - Vocabulary

Going on a Hike

Circle the list words in these sentences. Spell the list words aloud. Write the sentences on a separate sheet of paper.

1. A compass and sunglasses are important items to take on a hike.

2. The boys checked their watches to see when they had to return to camp.

3. The hikers attended classes on woodsman- ship before going into the forest.

4. The boys set up camp in a circle of bushes.

5. Jim cut a dead branch to use in the fire.

6. The other boys collected dry brush for kindling to start the campfire.

7. An air mattress makes sleeping on the ground more comfortable.

WORD LIST

compass
boxes
index
classes
churches
wrench
bushes
eyelash
mattress
radishes
foxes
brush
sunglasses
branch
crashes
punches
rashes
reflex
waxes
watches

LESSON 2 - Practice

1. Study the word list for Unit 6. Understand the meaning of each word.
2. Write each word twice on a separate paper.

LESSON 3 - Spelling Guide

> The plural of nouns ending with '-ss,' '-x,' '-ch' or '-sh' is formed by adding '-es.'

1. Write the plural form of these nouns.

wrench	bush	eyelash	mattress
_____	_____	_____	_____
radish	punch	rash	reflex
_____	_____	_____	_____
wax	watch	fox	brush
_____	_____	_____	_____
sunglass	branch	crash	compass
_____	_____	_____	_____
box	index	class	church
_____	_____	_____	_____

NOTE: The plural of index may also be spelled: indices.

2. Write all the words in your word list one more time on a separate paper.

24

LESSON 4 - Exercise

1. Write all the list words that are singular.

_____

_____

_____

_____

_____

_____

_____

2. Write all the list words that are plural.

_____

_____

_____

_____

_____

_____

_____

_____

_____

_____

NOTE: 'Sunglasses' does not usually have a singular form.

3. Take your first practice test on all words in the Unit 6 word list.

LESSON 5

Review your word list and take your final test. Write the words in the spaces provided at the back of this book. Remember to ask God for His help.

UNIT 7

WORD ENDINGS

LESSON 1 - Vocabulary

Fun at the Amusement Park

Circle the list words in these sentences. Spell the list words aloud. Write the sentences on a separate sheet of paper.

1. The musical carrousel is always a favorite ride at the amusement park.

2. Caramel apples and caramel corn are treats you can get at the park.

3. Mike likes to use the rifle at the shooting gallery.

4. Mom and Dad ride the paddle boats on the park's pond.

5. The model train chugs through a tunnel.

6. The Ferris wheel hardly ever stands idle.

7. The final ride of the day was the roller coaster.

WORD LIST

model
camel
caramel
cripple
carrousel
metal
meddle
final
musical
rifle
puzzle
single
signal
struggle
loyal
idle
idol
riddle
paddle
tunnel

LESSON 2 - Practice

1. Study the word list for Unit 7. Understand the meaning of each word.
2. Write each word twice on a separate paper.

LESSON 3 - Spelling Guide

> The unstressed /- əl/ ending may be spelled four ways: '-el,' '-le,' '-al' or '-ol.'
> Many common two-syllable English words have these unstressed endings in which the final sound is that of the letter 'l' with only a slight vowel sound.
>
> **NOTE: Three of your Unit 7 list words have '-el' or '-al' endings that are regular syllables with vowel sounds, not the unstressed endings that are found in the other words. (See exercise 2 below.)**

1. Complete these two-syllable list words by adding the correct form of the unstressed /- əl/ ending. Choose '-el,' '-le,' '-al' or -'ol.'

a. cripp____   j. puzz____
b. cam____   k. strugg____
c. mod____   l. sing____
d. rif____   m. sign____
e. fin____   n. id____
f. met____   o. id____
g. medd____   p. ridd____
h. loy____   q. padd____
i. tunn____

2. Complete these three-syllable list words by adding the correct ending. Choose '-el' or '-al.'

a. caram____   b. carrous____

c. music____

3. Write all the words in your word list one more time on a separate paper.

LESSON 4 - Exercise

1. Write all the list words with double consonants.

_____ _____

_____ _____

_____ _____

_____

2. Two words on your Unit 7 word list sound exactly alike but have slightly different spellings and completely different meanings. These are: 'idle' and 'idol.' Find their meanings in the mini-dictionary below and write the two words here for practice. Carefully study the differences in spelling.

_____ _____

3. Two words on your list have similar sounds but different spellings and different meanings. These are 'metal' and 'meddle.' Find their meanings in the mini-dictionary below and write the two words here for practice. Carefully study the spelling differences and listen for the different consonant sounds in the middle of each word.

_____ _____

4. Two words on your list are often confused because their spellings are so close. They are pronounced differently and have different meanings. These are 'single' and 'signal.' Find their meanings in the mini-dictionary below and write the two words here for practice. Notice the differences.

_____ _____

MINI-DICTIONARY

idle - doing nothing; not working; lazy.
idol - an image that is worshiped.

meddle - to interfere with other people's business.
metal - a solid substance which conducts electricity and can be shaped.

signal - a sign that a certain action should be taken.
single - being of only one form or part.

---

5. Take your first practice test on all words in the Unit 7 word list.

LESSON 5

Review your word list and take your final test. Write the words in the spaces provided at the back of this book. Remember to ask God for His help.

UNIT 8

PLURAL WORD ENDINGS

LESSON 1 - Vocabulary

Making Music

Circle the list words in these sentences. Spell the list words aloud. Write the sentences on a separate sheet of paper.

1. Tim practices his music lessons in a studio.

2. Cathy is learning to play the piano.

3. The low range for a woman's singing voice is called alto.

4. A woman with a high singing voice is a soprano.

5. Groups of three singers or instrumentalists are called trios.

6. The banjo is a happy sounding stringed instrument of the guitar family.

7. Do you have any heroes who are musicians?

WORD LIST

studio
potatoes
piano
alto
heroes
embargoes
motto
tobacco
tornado
buffalo
echoes
soprano
cameos
trios
banjo
domino
halo
tomatoes
calico
poncho

LESSON 2 - Practice

1. Study the word list for Unit 8. Understand the meaning of each word.
2. Write each word twice on a separate paper.

LESSON 3 - Spelling Guide

> Nouns ending with '-o' preceded by a vowel add '-s' to form their plurals.
>
> Most nouns ending with '-o' preceded by a consonant add '-s' to form the plural. However, there are many exceptions: many nouns ending with '-o' form their plurals by adding '-es.' You must memorize the correct spelling.
>
> There are other nouns ending with '-o' whose plurals may be formed with either '-s' or '-es.' Modern American English usage usually prefers simply adding '-s' to form the plural of these nouns.

1. The plural of these nouns is formed by adding only an 's.' Write the plural form in the blank following the word. (Write the whole word, not just the ending.)

studio _____   soprano _____

piano _____   trio _____

alto _____   poncho _____

cameo _____

2. The plural of these nouns is formed by adding '-es.' Write the plural form in the blanks. (Write the whole word.)

potato_____   echo_____

hero_____   tomato_____

embargo_____

3. Thinking about spelling: Why do the plurals of 'studio,' 'cameo' and 'trio' need only an '-s'? Check the Spelling Guide above for the answer.

4. Write all the words in your word list one more time on a separate paper.

30

1. The plural of these list words may be spelled by adding '-s' or '-es.' Write the list words. Write them again using both plural spellings.

	singular	plural with 's' (preferred)	plural with 'es'
motto	_____	_____	_____
tobacco	_____	_____	_____
tornado	_____	_____	_____
buffalo	_____	_____	_____
banjo	_____	_____	_____
domino	_____	_____	_____
halo	_____	_____	_____
calico	_____	_____	_____

2. Find the word 'motto' in a dictionary and learn the meaning. In the box below, write a motto for your life today. Write the word 'Motto' in the title blank.

My _____ for Today

3. Write a list word that has the letter in the DOMINO square.

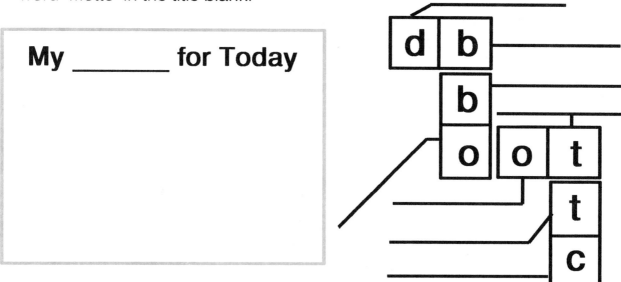

4. Take your first practice test on all words in the Unit 8 word list.

LESSON 5

Review your word list and take your final test. Write the words in the spaces provided at the back of this book. Remember to ask God for His help.

THE 'ONE-PLUS-ONE' RULE

LESSON 1 - Vocabulary

Roommates

Circle the list words in these sentences. Spell the list words aloud. Write the sentences on a separate sheet of paper.

1. Brothers Mike and Jason get along well and make good roommates.

2. When you must share a room, there is no place for meanness.

3. Mike was dissatisfied with Jason's neatness, but he did not get angry about it.

4. It is best not to overreact when your room- mate does not always do things as you like.

5. Sometimes roommates have dissimilar ways of doing things.

6. Jason accidentally spilled cola on Mike's desk.

WORD LIST
dissatisfied
overrun
meanness
misspell
unnoticed
underrate
suddenness
coolly
cruelly
naturally
roommate
bathhouse
glowworm
bookkeeper
irregular
dissimilar
unnatural
accidentally
finally
overreact

LESSON 2 - Practice

1. Study the word list for Unit 9. Understand the meaning of each word.
2. Write each word twice on a separate paper.

LESSON 3 - Spelling Guide

> When a prefix ends with the same letter as the first letter of the base word, or when a base word ends with the same letter as the first letter of a suffix, both letters are included in the spelling. Examples: 'un-needed' or 'usual-ly.'
>
> The same rule applies when two words - the first ending with the same letter with which the second begins - are joined together in a compound word. Example: 'cat-tail.'

1. Form list words by joining these prefixes and base words. Using the Spelling Guide above, decide whether to use both the last letter of the prefix and the first letter of the base word.

dis + satisfied	under + rate	over + react
_____	_____	_____
over + run	ir + regular	dis + similar
_____	_____	_____
un + natural	un + noticed	mis + spell
_____	_____	_____

2. Form list words by joining these base words and suffixes. Use the Spelling Guide above to understand the correct spellings.

mean + ness	sudden + ness	cool + ly
_____	_____	_____
cruel + ly	natural + ly	final + ly
_____	_____	_____
accidental + ly		
_____		

3. Write all the words in your word list one more time on a separate paper.

LESSON 4 - Exercise

1. Form compound list words by joining the words below. Notice that the last letter of the first word is the same as the first letter of the second word.

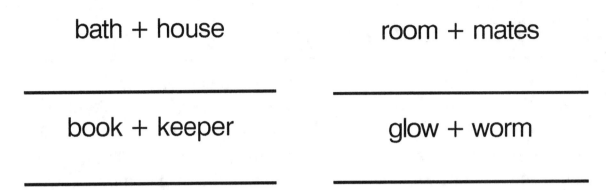

bath + house

room + mates

_____

_____

book + keeper

glow + worm

_____

_____

2. Draw an arrow from the base word on the left to the correct prefix or suffix. Write the <u>complete</u> list word you have formed in the blank.

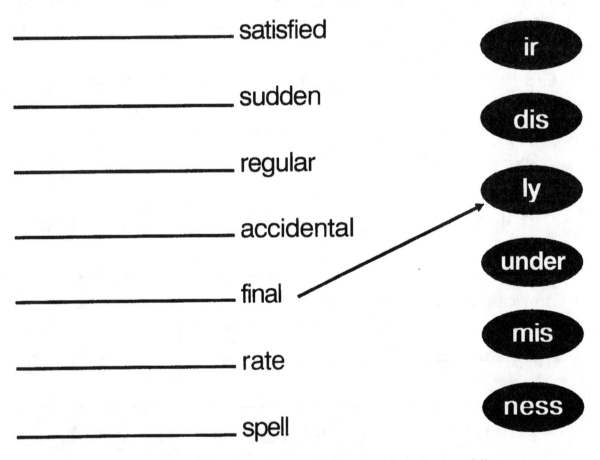

_____ satisfied

_____ sudden

_____ regular

_____ accidental

_____ final

_____ rate

_____ spell

ir

dis

ly

under

mis

ness

3. Take your first practice test on all words in the Unit 9 word list.

LESSON 5

Review your word list and take your final test. Write the words in the spaces provided at the back of this book. Remember to ask God for His help.

34

UNIT 10

SPELLING THE 'CH' SOUND

LESSON 1 - Vocabulary

Backyard Games

Circle the list words in these sentences. Spell the list words aloud. Write the sentences on a separate sheet of paper.

1. The boys in the neighborhood try to capture each other when they play soldiers.

2. Jack and Matt crouch in a ditch to hide from the "enemy soldiers."

3. The boys will charge up the field as they play flag football.

4. Jim is the pitcher for the baseball team and Mark is the catcher.

5. It is wrong to cheat when you play games.

6. In the future, some of the boys may grow up to be real soldiers or baseball players.

7. After playing, the boys have cookies in the kitchen at Randy's house.

WORD LIST

chapter
chance
catcher
picture
pitcher
charge
channel
ditch
stretch
scratch
future
nature
mixture
crouch
butcher
capture
bunch
kitchen
cheek
cheat

LESSON 2 - Practice

1. Study the word list for Unit 10. Understand the meaning of each word.
2. Write each word twice on a separate paper.

LESSON 3 - Spelling Guide

There are three ways to spell the 'ch' sound: 'ch,' 'tch' and 't.'

When 't' is used to spell the 'ch' sound, it is usually in combination with the letter 'u' (tu).

1. Group the Unit 10 list words according to the spelling of the 'ch' sound.

ch		tch	
	_____		_____
	_____		_____
	_____		_____
	_____		_____
	_____		_____
		t(u)	_____
	_____		_____
			_____
	_____		_____

2. Write all the words in your word list one more time on a separate paper.

1. Name the drawings below. Use 'pitcher' or 'picture.' Check a dictionary if necessary.

_____   _____   _____

2. Follow the clues to spell list words.

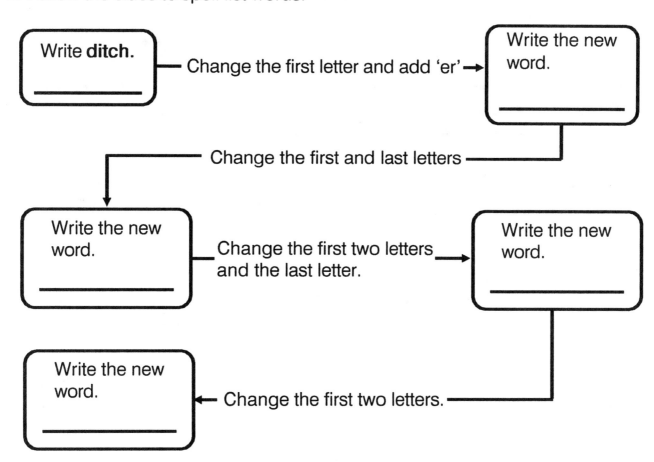

Write **ditch.**
_____

Change the first letter and add 'er' →

Write the new word.
_____

Change the first and last letters

Write the new word.
_____

Change the first two letters and the last letter. →

Write the new word.
_____

Write the new word.
_____

← Change the first two letters.

3. Take your first practice test on all words in the Unit 10 word list.

LESSON 5

Review your word list and take your final test. Write the words in the spaces provided at the back of this book. Remember to ask God for His help.

UNIT 11

REVIEW

LESSON 1 - Vocabulary

Thanksgiving

Circle the list words in this short story. Spell the list words aloud. Write the list words on a separate sheet of paper.

At last the harvest was all gathered in. The Pilgrims rejoiced as they saw the bountiful supply of food for the winter.... "Friends," said Governor Bradford, "God has blessed our summer's work, and has sent us a bountiful harvest. He brought us safe to this new home and protected us through the terrible winter. It is fit we have a time for giving thanks to God for His mercies to us. What say you? Shall we not have a week of feasting and of thanksgiving?"

"A week of thanksgiving!" said the Pilgrims. "Yes, let us rest from our work and spend the time in gladness and thanksgiving. God has been very good to us."

So it was decided that the next week should be set aside for the harvest feast of thanksgiving, and that their Indian friends should be asked to join them.

(From *Stories of the Pilgrims* by Margaret B. Pumphrey, copyright Christian Liberty Press)

WORD LIST
harvest
bountiful
governor
terrible
thanksgiving
protected
feasting
turkeys
gladness
Pilgrims
summer
winter
autumn
spring
rejoiced
delicious
ripened
cultivate
Indian
mercies

LESSON 2 - Practice

1. Study the word list for Unit 11. Understand the meaning of each word.
2. Write each word twice on a separate paper.

LESSON 3 - Spelling Guide

REVIEW - Study all the rules in the Lesson 3 Spelling Guides for each of the first 10 units of this book. Use some of the rules to complete these exercises.

1. Combine these base words and suffixes. Decide whether to keep or drop the final 'e' before adding the suffix.

rejoice + ed   cultivate + ing   give + ing

_____   _____   _____

2. Combine these base words and suffixes. Decide whether or not to double the last letter before adding the suffix.

protect + ed   feast + ing   ripen + ed

_____   _____   _____

3. Combine these base words and suffixes by applying the spelling rules you have learned so far.

bounty + ful   glad + ness   harvest + ing

_____   _____   _____

4. Chose the correct form of the unstressed ending syllable.

terrib____
-al
-le
-el
-ol

5. Write the correct plural form for each of these words.

Pilgrim _____
Indian _____
mercy _____
turkey _____

6. Write all the words in your word list one more time on a separate paper.

39

1. Which season of the year do you see in these pictures? Write the names of the seasons in the spaces. The season names are on your word list.

_____

_____

_____

_____

2. Choose list words to fill in the blanks.

   The food at the Th_____ feast was d_____. The P_____ invited their l_____ friends to join in the f_____. The Indians brought wild t_____ and berries which had r_____d in the s_____r sun. The Indians had taught the Pilgrims how to c_____ corn. The great feast was held in the a_____, which is the season of h_____. The Pilgrims r_____d with g_____ in their hearts because of God's great m_____ shown to them during the year.

3. Take your first practice test on all words in the Unit 11 word list.

LESSON 5

Review your word list and take your final test. Write the words in the spaces provided at the back of this book. Give thanksgiving to God for His help.

UNIT 12

WORD ENDINGS

LESSON 1 - Vocabulary

An Ocean Cruise

Circle the list words in these sentences. Spell the list words aloud. Write the sentences on a separate sheet of paper.

1. Grandpa and Grandma took a voyage on a cruise ship.

2. The place where the captain drives the ship is called the bridge.

3. The passengers' luggage was brought to their rooms by the ship's crew.

4. Another name for suitcases is baggage.

5. To send a message to someone on a ship you must use a radio.

6. Grandma put a postage stamp on the post card she sent us from a faraway country.

7. Grandpa and Grandma learned a foreign language before going on their journey.

WORD LIST

wedge
bridge
package
baggage
voyage
badge
bandage
wreckage
fudge
average
luggage
message
postage
ridge
language
courage
judge
passage
storage
dodge

LESSON 2 - Practice

1. Study the word list for Unit 12. Understand the meaning of each word.
2. Write each word twice on a separate paper.

LESSON 3 - Spelling Guide

There are two ways to spell the final 'j' sound: '-age' and '-dge.' You cannot tell from the sound which to use. You must memorize the correct spelling.

1. Choose '-age' or '-dge' to complete these list words.

do_____   bagg_____   langu_____
wreck_____   ju_____   fu_____
we_____   voy_____   ri_____
stor_____   cour_____   aver_____
bri_____   ba_____   post_____
pass_____   band_____   lugg_____
pack_____   mess_____

2. Write all list words with '-dge.'

_____
_____
_____
_____
_____
_____
_____

3. Write all list words with '-age.'

_____   _____
_____   _____
_____   _____
_____   _____
_____   _____
_____   _____
_____

4. Write all the words in your word list one more time on a separate paper.

42

1. Write the list words that fit the clues.

    a. A policeman has one. _____

    b. It spans a river. _____

    c. You need it in a time of danger. _____

    d. The fee for mailing something. _____

    e. What is left after a car accident. _____

    f. A flavor of ice cream toppings. _____

    g. Usual or common; in the middle. _____

    h. You speak it everyday. _____

    i. An idea you tell to someone. _____

2. Unscramble the letters to make list words. (Reminder: all words in this unit end with 'dge' or 'age.')

gluggea _____   ravegea _____

gabegag _____   crewkega _____

gedir _____   ganulaeg _____

jegdu _____   gadnabe _____

3. Take your first practice test on all words in the Unit 12 word list.

LESSON 5

Review your word list and take your final test. Write the words in the spaces provided at the back of this book. Pray for God's help with your test.

UNIT 13

SPELLING COMPUTER TERMS

LESSON 1 - Vocabulary

All About Computers

Circle the list words in these sentences. Spell the list words aloud. Write the sentences on a separate sheet of paper. The meanings of other list words are explained in Lesson 3.

1. A computer is a modern machine that stores and uses information to help us with many kinds of work.

2. A monitor is a television set attached to a computer to show information, pictures or words the computer is using.

3. A keyboard has buttons with letters and numbers and is used by people to put information into computers.

4. A printer is a machine which takes words and pictures from a computer and puts them on paper.

WORD LIST

computer
monitor
screen
keyboard
printer
disk
diskette
bit
byte
megabyte
software
hardware
memory
mouse
program
scanner
graphics
processor
drive
floppy

LESSON 2 - Practice

1. Study the word list for Unit 13. Understand the meaning of each word.
2. Write each word twice on a separate paper.

LESSON 3 - Spelling Guide

Many computers have operations that include a built-in dictionary. By using this dictionary, the computer can automatically check your spelling and make corrections if you spell words wrong. Since people do not do all of their writing on computers, it is important to learn how to spell in the usual way.

1. Write the list words that name the parts of the computer shown below.

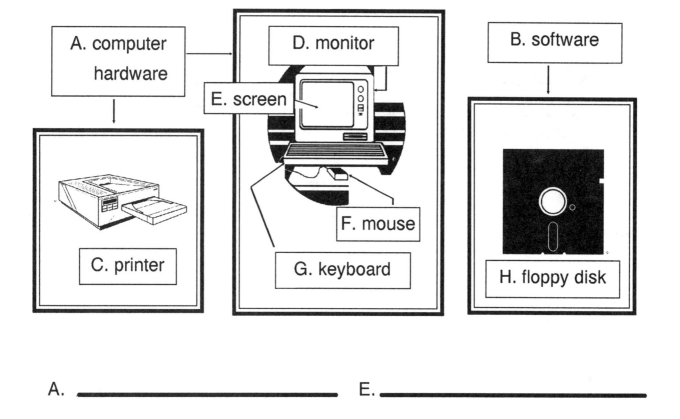

A. computer hardware

D. monitor

B. software

E. screen

F. mouse

C. printer

G. keyboard

H. floppy disk

A. _____   E. _____

B. _____   F. _____

C. _____   G. _____

D. _____   H. _____

LESSON 3 - (continued)

MINI-DICTIONARY

bit - a single electrical pulse or piece of electronic information used by a computer.

byte - a small group of bits which a computer calculates as a unit.

digital - relating to calculation by numbers. Computers work on information as if it were in the form of numbers.

disk - a round, flat, metal plate coated with a magnetic substance upon which a computer stores information.

diskette (floppy disk) - a small, flexible plastic disk coated with magnetic material upon which information can be stored for a computer.

drive - a part of a computer which operates a disk or diskette.

floppy - see diskette.

hardware - the machines that make up a computer system.

megabyte - approximately one-thousand bytes.

memory - the part of a computer that stores information for current or later use.

mouse - a hand-held pointing device connected to a computer that guides a pointer to different areas of a monitor screen.

processor - the part of a computer that calculates information for the user.

program - electronically coded instructions, stored on a disk or diskette, telling a computer how to operate or perform tasks.

scanner - a device which copies words or pictures and stores them in a computer's memory.

software - computer programs.

2. Write all the words in your word list one more time on a separate paper.

LESSON 4 - Exercise

1. Some computer terms have other meanings in ordinary English usage. Write these list words and find other meanings in a dictionary.

monitor_____: _____

_____

memory _____: _____

_____

program _____: _____

_____

drive _____: _____

_____

2. Take your first practice test on all words in the Unit 13 word list.

LESSON 5

Review your word list and take your final test. Write the words in the spaces provided at the back of this book. Pray for God's help with your test.

UNIT 14

WORDS WITH 'IE' AND 'EI'

LESSON 1 - Vocabulary

God Saves Jerusalem
(2 Chronicles 32)

Circle the list words in these sentences. Spell the list words aloud. Write the sentences on a separate sheet of paper.

1. During the reign of King Hezekiah, the city of Jerusalem was attacked by Assyria.

2. The king of Assyria and his army laid siege on Jerusalem.

3. Hezekiah and the people of Judah were willing to believe that God would save them.

4. The people of Judah would not yield to the wicked king of Assyria.

5. They prayed to God for relief.

6. God sent an angel to kill all the Assyrian soldiers in the field outside Jerusalem.

7. With God's help, Judah was able to achieve victory without fighting a battle.

WORD LIST

believe
chief
field
niece
piece
siege
yield
conceit
conceive
receive
achieve
deceive
relief
eight
freight
neighbor
reign
veil
retrieve
weigh

LESSON 2 - Practice

1. Study the word list for Unit 14. Understand the meaning of each word.
2. Write each word twice on a separate paper.

LESSON 3 - Spelling Guide

Memorize this poem to help you remember
how to spell words with 'ei' or 'ie':

Write 'i' before 'e'
Except after 'c',
Or when sounded as 'a'
as in 'neighbor' or 'weigh.'

This rule applies only when the pronunciation of 'ie' is a long 'e' as in
'he' or when 'ei' is pronounced as
long 'a' as in 'pale.'

Exceptions: neither, either, leisure, seize. Also, if the sound of 'ei' or 'ie' is
something other than long 'a' or 'e,' the rule does not apply, as in: science,
weird, conscience, fanciest or spicier.

1. Write all the list words in which 'i' comes before 'e.'

_____

_____

_____

_____

_____

_____

_____

_____

2. Write all the list words in which 'ei' comes after 'c.'

_____

_____

_____

_____

3. Write all the list words in which 'ei' is pronounced like long 'a.'

_____

_____

_____

_____

_____

4. Write all the words in your word list once more on separate paper.

48

LESSON 4 - Exercise

1. Write the two list words below.

chief_____

achieve_____

> Notice that in both of these words there is a 'c' before the 'ie.' The rule "'e' before 'i' when after 'c'" applies only when the vowel combination comes <u>immediately</u> after a 'c.'

2. Write the two words below.

siege_____

seize_____

> The list word 'siege' follows the 'ie' rule. The word 'seize' is an exception. To help you remember which is which, use this memory helper: A si ege is when an army si ts before a city until it surrenders. To se ize something is to se t your hands upon it.

3. Complete these list words by filling in the blanks. Choose 'ie' or 'ei.'

retr__ve	s__ge	ach__ve	p__ce
rec__ve	y__ld	dec__ve	n__ce
rel__f	f__ld	__ght	ch__f
conc__t	bel__ve	v__l	r__gn
conc__ve	n__ghbor	w__gh	fr__ght

4. Take your first practice test on all words in the Unit 14 word list.

LESSON 5

Review your word list and take your final test. Write the words in the spaces provided at the back of this book. Pray for God's help with your test.

49

UNIT 15

FINAL 'Y' - EXCEPTIONS

LESSON 1 - *Vocabulary*

A Princess Is Born

Circle the list words in these sentences. Spell the list words aloud. Write the sentences on a separate sheet of paper.

1. Once upon a time, her ladyship, the queen, had a baby girl.

2. The queen laid the new princess in her cradle and said, "I love you."

3. The king look skyward and thanked God for the little child.

4. There was much busyness around the castle on the day the princess was presented to the kingdom.

5. The princess was treated royally during her babyhood.

6. The people of the kingdom brought gifts to the castle daily.

WORD LIST

shyness
shyly
wryly
dryness
dryly
ladyship
ladylike
babyhood
babylike
busyness
business
paid
said
laid
slain
slyness
slyly
citylike
skyward
daily

LESSON 2 - Practice

1. Study the word list for Unit 15. Understand the meaning of each word.
2. Write each word twice on a separate paper.

LESSON 3 - Spelling Guide

Words ending in 'y' preceded by a consonant usually change 'y' to 'i' before before any suffix is added, except one beginning with 'i.' Another exception is for certain one-syllable adjectives with the suffixes '-ly' and '-ness.' Also, there is an exception to the usual rule for certain words with the suffixes '-ship,' '-like,' '-ward' and '-hood.'

Words ending in 'y' preceded by a vowel usually do not change 'y' to 'i' before adding suffixes or endings. Exceptions include the words: *lay, say, pay, slay, and day.* When '-ing' is added to some of these words, the usual rule is followed and the exception does not apply.

1. Form new words by adding the suffixes shown to these words.

	-ly	**-ness**
shy	_____	_____
wry	_____	_____
dry	_____	_____
sly	_____	_____

2. Form list words by adding suffixes to these words. Choose suffixes '-ship,' '-hood,' '-like' or '-ward.'

lady	_____	_____
baby	_____	_____
city	_____	
sky	_____	

3. Thinking about spelling: Did you change the 'y" before adding the endings? Why not? Study the Spelling Guide for the answer.

4. Write all the words in your word list one more time on separate paper.

1. Write a past form (past tense or past perfect tense) of these words. Check your word list for the correct spelling. Than write the words again, adding the '-ing' ending. Decide whether or not to change the 'y.'

Past Form	**-ing**
say _____	_____
pay _____	_____
lay _____	_____
slay (has)_____	_____

2. Write these two list words and study the different meanings in the boxes.

busyness   business

_____   _____

MEANING AND SPELLING	MEANING AND SPELLING
busyness (bĭz' - ē - nəs), noun - the state or condition of being busy.	business (bĭz'-nəs), noun - one's occupation; trade; commerce.
The spelling keeps the 'y' of 'busy' as an exception to the usual rule for 'y' endings and to avoid confusion with the word 'business.'	The word is made up of the root 'busy' and the suffix '-ness.' The 'y' is changed according to the usual rule. The 'i' is silent.

3. Take your first practice test on all words in the Unit 15 word list.

LESSON 5

Review your word list and take your final test. Write the words in the spaces provided at the back of this book. Pray for God's help with your test.

UNIT 16

WORDS WITH 'WH'

LESSON 1 - Vocabulary

Whistle or Whine?

Circle the list words in these sentences. Spell the list words aloud. Write the sentences on a separate sheet of paper.

1. Whistle while you work.

2. To whine about work is a kind of rebellion against God.

3. Do your work wholeheartedly, as an offering to God.

4. Whoever does not work, shall not eat.

5. Whose servant are you?

6. Put yourself wholly into your studies, and you will be rewarded with knowledge.

7. Set your mind on wholesome thoughts.

8. Whenever we complain, we lose some of the joy of the Lord.

WORD LIST

whoever
whole
wholesale
whom
whose
whomever
wholesome
wholly
wholehearted
whoop
whereas
whenever
which
whine
whirl
whiplash
whitewash
whittle
whisper
whistle

LESSON 2 - Practice

1. Study the word list for Unit 16. Understand the meaning of each word.
2. Write each word twice on a separate paper.

LESSON 3 - Spelling Guide

> The consonant digraph 'wh' at the beginning of words stands for three possible sounds:
>
> 1. 'wh' = 'h' This pronunciation is limited to words which are a form of or begin with 'who' and 'whole.'
> 2. 'wh' = 'hw' } 'Wh' in all other words may be pronounced either
> 3. 'wh' = 'w'   } of these two ways; 'hw' is preferred.
>
> In the word 'whoop,' the 'wh' may be pronounced 'h,' 'w,' or 'hw.'

1. Write all list words which begin with the 'h' sound of 'wh.'

_____   _____

_____   _____

_____   _____

_____   _____

_____

2. Write all list words which begin with the 'hw' or 'w' sound of 'wh.' (Do not include 'whoop.')

_____   _____

_____   _____

_____   _____

_____   _____

3. Write the list word in which the 'wh' may be pronounced any of the three ways: _____

4. Write all the words in your word list one more time on separate paper.

LESSON 4 - Exercise

1. Write sentences that include some form of these list words.

whisper   _____

_____

whittle   _____

_____

whenever _____

_____

whereas   _____

_____

whoever   _____

_____

whomever _____

_____

whose   _____

_____

whirl   _____

_____

whitewash _____

_____

whiplash   _____

_____

whistle   _____

_____

2. Take your first practice test on all words in the Unit 16 word list.

LESSON 5

Review your word list and take your final test. Write the words in the spaces provided at the back of this book. Pray for God's help with your test.

UNIT 17

THREE SOUNDS OF 'CH'

LESSON 1 - Vocabulary

Christian Character

Circle the list words in these sentences. Spell the list words aloud. Write the sentences on a separate sheet of paper.

1. Character is a person's moral condition or reputation.

2. Having a Christian character is to be Christlike and to be controlled by the Holy Spirit.

3. Even children can learn to show the love of Christ.

4. Being cheerful, kind, joyful, helpful and patient are signs of Christian character.

5. It is a challenge to love and forgive others when they do evil to us.

6. A true champion is one who is humble in victory.

WORD LIST

choir
chorus
stomach
echo
chronic
chronicle
Christian
mechanical
christen
chrome
character
children
challenge
chocolate
champion
cheerful
machine
chandelier
chauffeur
chivalry

LESSON 2 - Practice

1. Study the word list for Unit 17. Understand the meaning of each word.
2. Write each word twice on a separate paper.

LESSON 3 - Spelling Guide

> Three sounds in English words are spelled with the consonant digraph 'ch':
>
> Examples: The 'ch' in 'child' is pronounced 'tsh' as in 'church.'
> The 'ch' in 'echo' is pronounced 'k' as in 'kite.'
> The 'ch' in 'machine' is pronounced 'sh' as in 'wish.'

1. Write all the list words in which 'ch' stands for the sound of 'k.'

_____

_____

_____

_____

_____

_____

_____

_____

_____

2. Write all the list words in which 'ch' stands for the sound of 'sh.'

_____

_____

_____

3. Write all list words in which 'ch' stands for the sound 'tsh.'

_____

_____

_____

_____

_____

4. Write all the words in your word list one more time on separate paper.

1. Cross out one word in each group which does not belong. Write the list
   word or words from each group in the spaces provided.

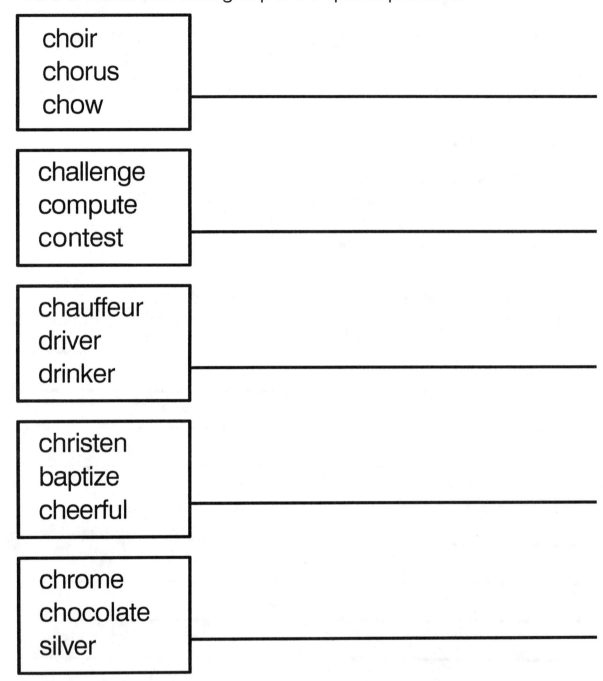

choir
chorus
chow

challenge
compute
contest

chauffeur
driver
drinker

christen
baptize
cheerful

chrome
chocolate
silver

2. Take your first practice test on all words in the Unit 17 word list.

LESSON 5

Review your word list and take your final test. Write the words in the spaces
provided at the back of this book. Pray for God's help with your test.

UNIT 18

SPELLING THE SOUND OF 'F'

LESSON 1 - Vocabulary

My Fantastic Family

**Circle all words with the sound of 'f.'
Spell the list words aloud. Write the
sentences on a separate sheet of paper.**

1. Members of my family can do fantastic things.

2. My uncle shot an elephant on safari in Africa.

3. My brother plays flute in a symphony orchestra.

4. My father has a trophy for catching the most fabulous fish in the world.

5. My mother had her photograph taken with the fancy queen of Freedonia.

6. I could say the alphabet when I was still an infant.

7. Do you think my family is fascinating or a fantasy?

WORD LIST

alphabet
elephant
geography
telephone
trophy
phonics
symphony
photograph
phonograph
hyphen
philosophy
pharmacy
physical
physician
family
fantasy
infant
fabulous
fascinating
fantastic

LESSON 2 - Practice

1. Study the word list for Unit 18. Understand the meaning of each word.
2. Write each word twice on a separate paper.

LESSON 3 - Spelling Guide

> The sound of 'f' in English words may be spelled in two ways: 'f' and 'ph.'

1. Write all the list words in which 'ph' stands for the 'f' sound.

_____   _____

_____   _____

_____   _____

_____   _____

_____   _____

_____   _____

_____   _____

2. Write all the list words in which 'f' stands for the 'f' sound.

_____   _____

_____   _____

_____   _____

3. Memory helpers: Memorize these sentences. Write the first letter of each word in the blanks to form hard-to-spell list words.

George Edwards' old grandmother rode a pig home yesterday.

___ ___ ___ ___ ___ ___ ___ ___

Some young men play horns on New Year's.

___ ___ ___ ___ ___ ___ ___ ___

4. Write all the words in your word list one more time on separate paper.

At the top of each page in a dictionary, there are guide words showing the first and last word on that page. When looking up a word, find the page on which your word comes alphabetically between the guide words.

1. Below are several sets of guide words. Write a list word that would come on a page with these guide words. Choose from the list below ⟶

   Example:

allow   alpine
alphabet

faith   famous
_____

   infant

trod   trouble
_____

elegance   elite
_____

   elephant

   trophy

fancy   farm
_____

industry   infer
_____

   pharmacy

   fantasy

phrase   piano
_____

phantom   phase
_____

   physical

   family

2. Look up these list words in a dictionary. Use the guide words on the dictionary page to help you find them. Write a short definition for each word on a separate paper.

philosophy	phonics	fabulous
physician	fantastic	geography

3. Take your first practice test on all words in the Unit 18 word list.

LESSON 5

Review your word list and take your final test. Write the words in the spaces provided at the back of this book. Ask God for his help with your test.

UNIT 19

WORD ENDINGS

LESSON 1 - Vocabulary

Are You 'Able' to Spell Big Words?

Circle all list words in these sentences. Spell the list words aloud. Write the sentences on a separate sheet of paper.

1. My dog is a very lovable pet.

2. There are many famous places to visit in the eastern part of our country.

3. The cowboys were pleased to see how peaceable the wild horse had become.

4. My Aunt Maggie is an excitable person.

5. The weather is changeable in the spring.

6. Our sins are not excusable, but they may be forgiven.

7. It is a blessing to live a virtuous life.

WORD LIST

advantageous
desirous
admirable
changeable
deplorable
courageous
famous
noticeable
imaginary
outrageous
lovable
peaceable
movable
serviceable
unimaginable
embraceable
traceable
excitable
excusable
virtuous

LESSON 2 - Practice

1. Study the word list for Unit 19. Understand the meaning of each word.
2. Write each word twice on a separate paper.

LESSON 3 - Spelling Guide

> Words ending in silent '-e' usually drop the '-e' before a suffix beginning with a vowel is added.
>
> But if a 'c' or 'g' comes just before final silent '-e,' the '-e' is kept if the suffix begins with 'a' or 'o.' This also indicates the soft sound of 'c' or 'g.'

1. Combine these word parts to form list words. Decide whether or not to keep the final silent '-e.'

outrage + ous _____   advantage + ous _____

love + able _____   virtue + ous _____

imagine + ary _____   desire + ous _____

peace + able _____   excuse + able _____

notice + ably _____   admire + able _____

move + able _____   excite + able _____

fame + ous _____   change + able _____

service + able _____   trace + able _____

courage + ous _____   deplore + able _____

un+imagine+ _____   embrace + able _____
    able

2. Thinking about spelling:
    a. Did you drop final '-e' from move before adding '-able'? Why or why not?
    b. Did you drop final '-e' from fame before adding '-ous'? Why or why not?
    c. Did you drop final '-e' from trace before adding '-able'? Why or why not?

3. Write all the words in your word list one more time on separate paper.

Most of the list words in this unit are big words. But big does not always mean difficult. When learning how to spell big words, here are some ways to make them seem easier:

1. Break the word into smaller parts.
2. Find the base word, if there is one.
3. Find suffixes, prefixes, beginnings, endings and syllables.
4. Use spelling rules to decide if the base word is changed in any way before other parts are added. Also remember phonics rules.
5. Put the parts back together to see how the whole word looks and sounds.

1. Break these words into smaller parts. Place hyphens (-) between important word parts. Show where silent '-e' is or normally would be on base words by using parentheses (e) around the 'e' or missing 'e.'

Example:

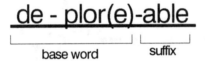

de - plor(e)-able

base word   suffix

embraceable   unimaginable

_____   _____

advantageous   admirable

_____   _____

noticeably   serviceable

_____   _____

2. Take your first practice test on all words in the Unit 19 word list.

LESSON 5

Review your word list and take your final test. Write the words in the spaces provided at the back of this book. Ask God for his help with your test.

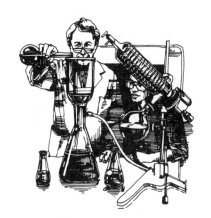

UNIT 20

WORD ENDINGS

LESSON 1 - Vocabulary

When We Grow Up

Circle all list words in these sentences. Spell the list words aloud. Write the sentences on a separate sheet of paper.

1. Richard wants to be a dentist when he grows up. Jim wants to be a counselor.

2. If I practice my piano lessons well, I can become even a greater pianist.

3. My sister is a secretary, and she is an excellent typist.

4. Jennifer enjoys nature and would like to become a scientist when she is older.

5. My mother is the prettiest one in our neighborhood. I think I would be happiest if I become a mother someday also.

6. John wants to be a movie actor and director when he grows up.

WORD LIST

voyager
freezer
greater
uglier
brighter
warrior
director
actor
counselor
survivor
happiest
gloomiest
prettiest
loudest
quietest
typist
pianist
dentist
scientist
soloist

LESSON 2 - Practice

1. Study the word list for Unit 20. Understand the meaning of each word.
2. Write each word twice on a separate paper.

LESSON 3 - Spelling Guide

The suffixes '-er' and '-or' mean someone or something that does something. Examples:

A washer is a machine that washes.
An inspector is someone who inspects things.

The suffix '-ist' also means someone who does something. Example:

A violinist is someone who plays the violin.

The suffixes '-er' and '-est' are added to adjectives to show comparison. The suffix '-er' means more; '-est' means most. Examples:

green   -   greener   -   greenest
noisy   -   noisier   -   noisiest

1. Choose a list word which goes with these definitions. Write the word.

a. someone who fights in a war _____

b. noisiest _____

c. someone who does dental (teeth) work _____

d. someone who plays the piano _____

e. someone who goes on a voyage _____

f. more unpleasant looking _____

g. most beautiful _____

h. someone who survived a mishap _____

i. someone who gives advice or counsel _____

j. someone who directs _____

2. Write all the words in your word list one more time on separate paper.

1. Choose '-er' or '-or' to complete these list words. Say the words aloud.

counsel____   surviv____   warri____   act____

voyag____   freez____   direct____

2. Choose '-est' or '-ist' to complete these list words. Say the words aloud.

typ____   happi____   pian____   quiet____

dent____   pretti____   solo____

gloomi____   scient____   loud____

3. Write list words that fit these comparisons.

ugly	_____	ugliest
pretty	prettier	_____
bright	_____	brightest
quiet	quieter	_____
happy	happier	_____
great	_____	greatest
gloomy	gloomier	_____
loud	louder	_____

4. Take your first practice test on all words in the Unit 20 word list.

LESSON 5

Review your word list and take your final test. Write the words in the spaces provided at the back of this book. Ask God for his help with your test.

UNIT 21

SIMILAR FORMS

LESSON 1 - Vocabulary

School Days

Circle all list words in these sentences. Spell the list words aloud. Write the sentences on a separate sheet of paper.

1. I enjoy my spelling course at school.

2. The principal of our school is a kind man, but he is firm with discipline.

3. We receive wonderful counsel from our teachers when we have problems.

4. My teacher has taught me to accept correction when I need it.

5. Our class took a trip to the capital city of our state, and we visited the capitol building.

6. The school secretary typed a letter on official school stationery.

7. We may not tell coarse jokes at school.

WORD LIST

accept
except
affect
effect
altar
alter
council
counsel
capital
capitol
principal
principle
coarse
course
stationary
stationery
complement
compliment
irrelevant
irreverent

68

LESSON 2 - Practice

1. Study the word list for Unit 21. Understand the meaning of each word.
2. Write each word twice on a separate paper.

LESSON 3 - *Spelling Guide*

> Learn the spelling differences between words similar or identical in sound but different in meaning.

1. Write your list words in the spaces below. Study and learn the meanings.

_____ **accept** - To take something offered; to believe

_____ **except** - To leave out; not including

_____ **affect** - To influence; to pretend

_____ **effect** - To make happen; a result; an outcome

_____ **altar** - A place of worship or sacrifice

_____ **alter** - To change

_____ **council** - A group called together for discussion

_____ **counsel** - Advice; to give advice; one who advises

_____ **capital** - Chief; the leading city; material wealth

_____ **capitol** - The central government building

_____ **principal** - Most important; the chief of a school

_____ **principle** - A truth; a belief; a rule to live by

_____ **coarse** - Rough; crude

_____ **course** - Path; direction; a program of study

_____ **stationary** - Not movable; not changing; fixed in place

_____ **stationery** - Writing paper

_____ **complement** - Something that completes

_____ **compliment** - Praise; an expression of admiration

_____ **irrelevant** - Not to the point

_____ **irreverent** - Lacking in reverence or respect

2. Write all the words in your word list one more time on separate paper.

LESSON 4 - Exercise

1. Memory helpers

   a. A capitOl building often has a dOme.

   b. A compLEment is something that compLEtes.

   A compLIment is a poLIte expression of praise.

   c. A principLE is a ruLE.

d. StationAry means 'in plAce.'

e. When we ACcept something we ACquire it.

When we EXcept something we 'X' it out or EXclude it.

2. Cross out the wrong word in the brackets. Write the correct word in the blank.

_____ a. The church [council / counsel] held a meeting on Monday night.

_____ b. Abraham built an [alter / altar] for a sacrifice to God.

_____ c. The [capital / capitol] of the United States is Washington, D.C.

_____ d. The Golden Rule is a good [principal / principle] by which to live.

_____ e. [Except / Accept] the Lord build the house, they labor in vain who build it (Psalm 127:1).

_____ f. It is [irrelevant / irreverent] to pop bubble gum during prayer time.

3. Take your first practice test on all words in the Unit 21 word list.

LESSON 5

Review your word list and take your final test. Write the words in the spaces provided at the back of this book. God will help if you have faithfully studied.

UNIT 22

SIMILAR FORMS

LESSON 1 - Vocabulary

Bible Wisdom

Circle all list words in these sentences. Spell the list words aloud. Write the sentences on a separate sheet of paper.

1. "Choose you this day whom ye will serve... we will serve the Lord" (Joshua 24:15).

2. "Lead me, O Lord, in thy righteousness... make thy way straight before my face" (Psalm 5:8).

3. "By the word of the Lord were the heavens made; and all the host of them by the breath of his mouth" (Psalm 33:6).

4. "For what is a man profited, if he shall gain the whole world and lose his own soul?" (Matthew 16:26).

5. "For we walk by faith, not by sight" (2 Corinthians 5:7).

6. "Except a man be born again, he cannot see the kingdom of God" (John 3:3).

7. "He that believeth not is condemned already" (John 3:18).

WORD LIST

choose
chose
loose
lose
formally
formerly
straight
strait
breath
breathe
all ready
already
cite
site
sight
born
borne
accent
ascent
assent

71

LESSON 2 - Practice

1. Study the word list for Unit 22. Understand the meaning of each word.
2. Write each word twice on a separate paper.

LESSON 3 - Spelling Guide

> Learn the spelling differences between words similar or identical in sound but different in meaning.

1. Write your list words in the spaces below. Study and learn the meanings.

_____ **choose** - To select; to pick out

_____ **chose** - Past tense of choose

_____ **loose** - Not fastened; not confined; careless

_____ **lose** - To fail to win; to misplace

_____ **formally** - In an outwardly correct manner

_____ **formerly** - Previously

_____ **straight** - Not curved; direct; upright

_____ **strait** - Narrow; strict; a narrow passage of water

_____ **breath** - Air drawn into the lungs

_____ **breathe** - To take a breath

_____ **all ready** - Everyone is ready.

_____ **already** - By this time

_____ **cite** - To quote; to use as an example

_____ **site** - Location; a place

_____ **sight** - Vision; to see

_____ **born** - Brought into life or being

_____ **borne** - Carried; endured

_____ **accent** - Emphasis or stress; to stress

_____ **ascent** - Climbing; a way up

_____ **assent** - To agree; agreement

2. Write all the words in your word list one more time on separate paper.

LESSON 4 - Exercise

1. Cross out the wrong word in the brackets. Write the correct word in the blank.

_____ a. My shoelaces are [lose / loose].

_____ b. The children were [all ready / already] to go home.

_____ c. Take a deep [breathe / breath] and then blow out the candles.

_____ d. It is dangerous to [breathe / breath] on people when you have a cold.

_____ e. Jesus has [born / borne] our sins to the cross.

_____ f. The [assent / ascent] up the mountain was difficult for the climbers.

_____ g. You can draw a [straight / strait] line with a ruler.

_____ h. She speaks quite [formally / formerly] when talking with the queen.

_____ i. The sailors hoped to [sight, cite] land after three months at sea.

_____ j. This is a good [site, cite] to pitch our tent.

_____ k. Abraham Lincoln was [born / borne] on February 12.

_____ l. This word has an [accent / assent] on the first syllable.

_____ m. I win; you [loose / lose]!

2. Take your first practice test on all words in the Unit 22 word list.

LESSON 5

Review your word list and take your final test. Write the words in the spaces provided at the back of this book. Pray for God's help with your test.

UNIT 23

WORD ENDINGS

LESSON 1 - Vocabulary

Solving a Mystery

Circle all list words in these sentences. Spell the list words aloud. Write the sentences on a separate sheet of paper.

1. It happened on a dark and stormy night.

2. The detective is traveling to the scene of the "crime."

3. The detective held a conference with everyone who was in the house at the time.

4. Who could have benefited from taking the missing items?

5. Everyone said someone else committed the terrible deed.

6. It was beginning to seem like a very difficult case to solve.

7. Finally, Billy admitted he took the cookies.

WORD LIST

admitted
beginning
committed
concurring
conferring
equipped
occurrence
submitted
compelled
preferred
controlled
benefited
profited
marvelous
traveling
happened
interpreted
reference
preference
conference

LESSON 2 - Practice

1. Study the word list for Unit 23. Understand the meaning of each word.
2. Write each word twice on a separate paper.

LESSON 3 - Spelling Guide

WHEW! YOU NEED A DETECTIVE TO FIGURE THAT RULE OUT!

When a word with two or more syllables:
- is accented on the last syllable, and
- ends with a single consonant preceded by a single vowel,
the final consonant is doubled before adding a suffix that:
- begins with a vowel.

EXAMPLE: con-fer' ----> con-fer(r)ed'

If adding a suffix to such a word <u>shifts the accent</u> to a syllable which is not the last syllable, the final consonant is not doubled before adding a suffix beginning with a vowel.

EXAMPLE: con-fer' ----> con'-fer-ence

1. Form list words by adding suffixes to these base words. Decide whether or not to double the final consonant on the base word.

confer + ing	submit + ed	prefer + ed
_____	_____	_____
confer + ence	refer + ence	prefer + ence
_____	_____	_____
marvel + ous	happen + ed	benefit + ed
_____	_____	_____
travel + ing	interpret +ed	control + ed
_____	_____	_____
compel + ed	begin + ing	admit +ed
_____	_____	_____

2. Write all the words in your word list one more time on separate paper.

LESSON 4 - Exercise

1. Use list words to complete this crossword puzzle.

1. Past tense of commit

2. Past tense of concur

3. A happening; something that has come about

4. Prepared with equipment

5. Surrendered; gave in

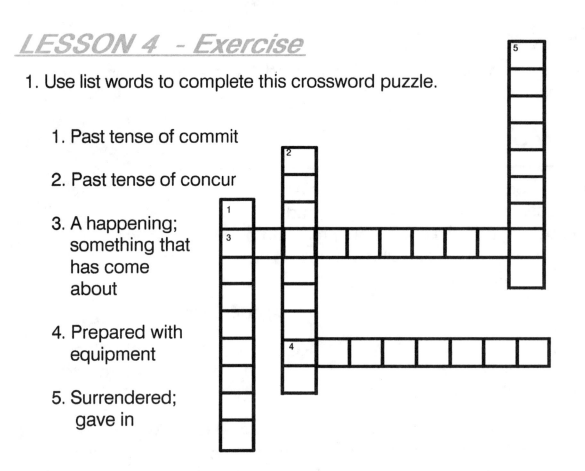

2. Choose one of the words at the right to complete the sentence.,

| submitted | a. The scouts were well _____ for their camping trip. |
| equipped | |

| conference | b. What is your _____ for dinner, meatloaf or spaghetti? |
| preference | |

| controlled | c. The forest fire has been _____ by brave firefighters. |
| admitted | |

| occurrence | d. This is the fourth _____ of flu in our class. |
| concurring | |

3. Take your first practice test on all words in the Unit 23 word list.

LESSON 5

Review your word list and take your final test. Write the words in the spaces provided at the back of this book. Pray for God's help with your test.

UNIT 24

REVIEW

LESSON 1 - Vocabulary

Circle all list words in these sentences.
Spell the list words aloud. Write the
sentences on a separate sheet of paper.

1. We cannot always have whatever we want.

2. A cool beverage is refreshing on a hot day.

3. My wagon has a broken wheel.

4. The ship was loaded with tons of cargo
   which had been stored on the wharf.

5. A warm fire and a soft quilt give me a
   feeling of coziness on a cold night.

6. I keep my favorite books on a ledge above
   my bed.

7. The president is the head of the executive
   branch of the federal government.

8. The sergeant had a chevron on the sleeve
   of his jacket.

WORD LIST

weight
grief
beverage
ledge
coziness
likelihood
whatever
wheel
wharf
whosoever
chastise
charity
chemistry
chevron
phony
pheasant
federal
fluoride
conqueror
communist

LESSON 2 - Practice

1. Study the word list for Unit 24. Understand the meaning of each word.
2. Write each word twice on a separate paper.

LESSON 3 - Spelling Guide

REVIEW - Study all the rules in the Lesson 3 Spelling Guides for Units 12-23. Use some of the rules to complete these exercises.

1. Write two list words in which 'ch' stands for the 'tch' sound.

   _____

   _____

   Write one list word in which 'ch' stands for the 'k' sound.

   _____

   Write one list word in which 'ch' stands for the 'sh' sound.

   _____

2. Write two list words in which the 'f' sound is spelled 'ph.'

   _____

   _____

   Write two list words in which the 'f' sound is spelled with 'f.'

   _____

   _____

3. Write three list words in which 'wh' stands for the 'hw' or 'w' sound.

   _____   _____   _____

   Write a list word in which 'wh' stands for 'h.'   _____

4. Choose '-dge' or 'age' to complete these list words.

   bever_____   le_____

5. Choose 'ie' or 'ei' to complete these list words.

   w____ght   gr____f

6. Form list words by combining these base words and suffixes.

   cozy+ness   like+ly+hood

   _____   _____

7. Write all the words in your word list one more time on separate paper.

78

LESSON 4 - Exercise

1. Write list words to fit these meanings.

_____ Someone who conquers

_____ Someone who believes in communism

_____ Scientific study of substances

_____ Fake

_____ It's found in many kinds of toothpaste

_____ A wild game bird

_____ Heaviness

_____ Probability

_____ Help for the poor

_____ To punish or scold

_____ Something to drink

_____ No matter what

_____ No matter which person

_____ Deep sadness or sorrow

_____ A dock where ships are loaded

_____ It rolls under a bicycle or car

What is this?

____ v ____

2. Take your first practice test on all words in the Unit 24 word list.

LESSON 5

Review your word list and take your final test. Write the words in the spaces provided at the back of this book. Pray for God's help with your test.

EXCELLENT

WORD ENDINGS

LESSON 1 - Vocabulary

What and Who?

Circle all list words in these sentences. Spell the list words aloud. Write the sentences on a separate sheet of paper.

1. The dentist's assistant handed him the tools he needed to clean my teeth.

2. The old mountaineer lived in a log cabin high in the Rockies.

3. The parking lot attendant collected fees from all drivers as they entered.

4. Jack is a resident of Minnesota and likes to go fishing.

5. Wildflowers were abundant in the sunny meadow.

6. Always do your most important work first.

7. George has been an excellent employee.

WORD LIST

employee
addressee
absentee
devotee
payee
mountaineer
puppeteer
engineer
volunteer
assistant
accountant
defendant
attendant
merchant
resident
frequent
excellent
abundant
important
lubricant

LESSON 2 - Practice

1. Study the word list for Unit 25. Understand the meaning of each word.
2. Write each word twice on a separate paper.

LESSON 3 - Spelling Guide

> The noun suffixes '-ee,' '-eer,' '-ent' and '-ant' usually mean 'one who.'
> The adjective suffixes '-ent' and '-ant' usually mean 'that which.'

1. Write a list word to fit the meaning.

_____ One who controls puppets

_____ One who works for wages

_____ One who assists

_____ One who works for free

_____ One who is defended

_____ That which is plentiful

_____ That which matters

_____ That which lubricates

_____ That which happens often

_____ One who is addressed

_____ One who is paid

_____ One who keeps accounts of money

_____ One who buys and sells goods

_____ One who is devoted to someone or something

2. Write all the words in your word list one more time on separate paper.

LESSON 4 - Exercise

1. Write a list word to fit the meaning.

_____ One who lives in or climbs mountains

_____ That which is exceptionally fine or good

_____ One who is not present

_____ One who controls an engine

_____ One who attends another to provide a service

_____ One whose home is in a particular place

2. Complete these sentences with list words.

a. If you climbed mountains in Glacier National Park, you would be
a _____.

b. If you were a teacher, you would be an _____ of a school.

c. If you lived in Paris, you would be a _____ of France.

d. If you give your time to an organization for free, you would be
considered a _____.

e. If it rains every day in the jungle, you could say that rain is a
_____ occurrence there.

f. If a great amount of rain falls in the jungle, you could say that the
rainfall is _____ there.

g. If your name and address are on a letter you receive, you are
the _____.

3. Take your first practice test on all words in the Unit 25 word list.

LESSON 5

Review your word list and take your final test. Write the words in the spaces
provided at the back of this book. Pray for God's help with your test.

UNIT 26

WORD ENDINGS

LESSON 1 - Vocabulary

Good Business

Circle all list words in these sentences. Spell the list words aloud. Write the sentences on a separate sheet of paper.

1. A good business is one that is profitable. and honoring to God.

2. A good business needs dependable workers.

3. If you are successful in business, it is possible to earn a comfortable living.

4. Having happy customers is a way by which the success of a business is measurable.

5. A business that is ably managed will probably grow.

6. A good location is a desirable asset for a business.

7. Cheating people is a contemptible business practice (Leviticus 19:35-37).

WORD LIST

possible
probably
dependable
visibly
sensibly
profitable
comfortable
edible
measurable
reasonable
ably
notable
eligible
legibly
desirable
contemptible
agreeable
terrible
unbelievable
livable

LESSON 2 - *Practice*

1. Study the word list for Unit 26. Understand the meaning of each word.
2. Write each word twice on a separate paper.

LESSON 3 - *Spelling Guide*

> The suffixes '-able' and '-ible may be added to base words or syllables to form adjectives. The suffixes '-ably' and '-ibly' may be added to base words or syllables to form adverbs.
>
> Base words ending in silent '-e' drop the '-e' before adding these suffixes unless the final '-e' is preceded by 'g' or 'c.' (Review Unit 19 Spelling Guide, page 63.)

> The suffixes '-able' and '-ible' usually mean 'full of' or 'able to be.'

1. Write list words to fit these meanings.

_____ Able to be depended upon

_____ Full of terror

_____ Able to agree

_____ Full of good reason

_____ Able to make or produce a profit

_____ Able to be measured

_____ Full of contempt

_____ Unable to be believed

_____ Able to be lived in

_____ Able to be desired

2. Write all the words in your word list one more time on separate paper.

The base word or syllable of some of your list words comes from the Latin language. By understanding the roots of word parts, we can sometimes better understand word meanings and spellings.

1. See if you can discover which list words are formed from these word parts.

_____ The Latin word *posse*, meaning 'to be able' + *ibilis*, Latin meaning 'able.' In English, this word means 'able to happen.'

_____ The Latin word *probare*, meaning 'to try, to test, to prove' +*abilis*, meaning 'able' in Latin. In English, this word is the adverb (-ly) form of a word meaning 'able to be supported by evidence.'

_____ The Latin word *visus*, meaning 'seen' + *ibilis*, meaning 'able.' In English, this word is the adverb (-ly) form of a word meaning 'able to be seen.'

_____ The Latin word *edere*, meaning 'to eat' + *ibilis*, meaning 'able.' In English, this word means 'able to be eaten.'

_____ The Latin word *eligere*, meaning 'to choose' + *ibilis*, meaning 'able.' In English, this word means 'able or qualified to be chosen.'

_____ The Latin word *sensus*, meaning 'felt or understood' + *ibilis*, meaning 'able.' In English this word means 'able to be understood.'

2. Take your first practice test on all words in the Unit 26 word list.

LESSON 5

Review your word list and take your final test. Write the words in the spaces provided at the back of this book. Pray for God's help with your test.

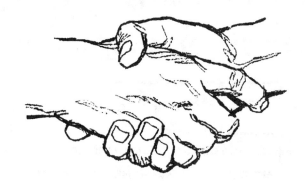

UNIT 27

COMPOUND WORDS

LESSON 1 - Vocabulary

When Words Get Together

Circle all list words in these sentences. Spell the list words aloud. Write the sentences on a separate sheet of paper.

1. Loud music gives Tim's mom a headache.

2. Ashley tripped on her shoelaces while she was walking down the hallway.

3. Mark went downtown to get a haircut.

4. Jennifer had a pancake and grapefruit for breakfast.

5. Mr. Barton read his newspaper on the airplane.

6. The astronauts landed their spaceship at a spaceport in California.

7. After the shipwreck, the old sailing vessel remained in its underwater grave.

WORD LIST

bookmark
shoelaces
shipwreck
hallway
headache
pancake
grapefruit
scorecard
airplane
shotgun
haircut
sunshine
spellbound
downstairs
floorboards
newspaper
saucepan
fingernail
spaceport
underwater

LESSON 2 - Practice

1. Study the word list for Unit 27. Understand the meaning of each word.
2. Write each word twice on a separate paper.

LESSON 3 - Spelling Guide

> A compound word is made up of two or more complete words joined to form a new word.

1. Separate the two words in these compound list words by writing the halves in the two boxes. Then write the words in the shaded boxes in Exercise 2.

2. Choose a word from the list at the right to join with the word in each shaded box below. This will form a new compound word which is not on your word list.

newspaper

underwater

scorecard

shipwreck

headache

bookmark

board

back

friend

melon

hymn

red

3. Write all the words in your word list one more time on separate paper.

1. Choose a word from Group A and a word from Group B to form compound words from your Unit 27 word list.

Group A	**Compound Words**	*Group B*
space	_____	laces
shoe	_____	way
finger	_____	cake
hall	_____	fruit
sauce	_____	plane
pan	_____	gun
floor	_____	cut
grape	_____	shine
down	_____	bound
air	_____	stairs
spell	_____	boards
shot	_____	pan
sun	_____	nail
hair	_____	port
	_____	

2. Take your first practice test on all words in the Unit 27 word list.

LESSON 5

Review your word list and take your final test. Write the words in the spaces provided at the back of this book. Ask God for His help with your test.

UNIT 28

WORD BEGINNINGS

LESSON 1 - Vocabulary

Before and After

Circle all list words in these sentences. Spell the list words aloud. Write the sentences on a separate sheet of paper.

1. The weather forecast calls for rain tonight.

2. Our forefathers were God-fearing men who founded our country on the Bible.

3. It would be premature to expect everyone to understand without further instruction.

4. We cannot fill your order without prepayment.

5. A pronoun must have an antecedent.

6. The doctor gave me medicine for a postnasal infection.

7. Much rebuilding was required during the postwar period.

WORD LIST

postpone
postwar
postscript
postdate
postnasal
forecast
forefathers
forewarn
forearm
foreknowledge
foreground
prepayment
predestination
precede
prelude
premature
prehistoric
antechamber
antedate
antecedent

LESSON 2 - Practice

1. Study the word list for Unit 28. Understand the meaning of each word.
2. Write each word twice on a separate paper.

LESSON 3 - Spelling Guide

> The prefixes 'fore-,' 'pre-' and 'ante-' mean 'before' or 'in front of.'
> The prefix 'post-' means 'behind' or 'after.'

1. Choose a list word which best fits the meaning.

a. after a war _____

b. to warn ahead of time _____

c. before history _____

d. a small room serving as an
    entry to a larger room _____

e. behind the nose _____

f. payment ahead of time _____

g. an area in front view _____

h. knowledge of something
    before it happens _____

i. the idea that God determines
    all things before they happen _____

j. the first or lower part of an arm _____

k. before being mature or complete _____

l. ancestors (fathers from earlier times) _____

3. Write all the words in your word list one more time on separate paper.

LESSON 4 - Exercise

1. Choose a list word that fits the description of the word's origin. Review the Lesson 3 Spelling Guide for the meanings of the prefixes.

WORD ROOTS   ENGLISH MEANING

post + ponere _____   to place after; to delay
↓
Latin: 'to place or put'

<hr />

ante + cedere _____   an earlier word to which a pronoun refers; something that goes before another thing
↓
Latin: 'to go'

<hr />

post + scribere _____   a short message written at the end of a letter
↓
Latin: 'to write'

<hr />

fore + casten _____   to plan or predict a future event; a prediction of something in the future
↓
Middle English: 'to plan; to cast'

2. Take your first practice test on all words in the Unit 28 word list.

LESSON 5

Review your word list and take your final test. Write the words in the spaces provided at the back of this book. Ask God for His help with your test.

UNIT 29

WORD BEGINNINGS

LESSON 1 - Vocabulary

Togetherness

Circle all list words in these sentences. Spell the list words aloud. Write the sentences on a separate sheet of paper.

1. I enjoy the company of my friends.

2. A friend is someone in whom you can place your confidence.

3. My friends and I like to cooperate with each other when we have work to do.

4. Christian friends enjoy communion with each other because they belong to Christ.

5. It is easy to communicate with a friend who understands how we think.

6. When a friend is in need, we must show compassion.

7. Our behavior should conform with the example which Jesus set for us.

WORD LIST

conserve
compete
company
cooperate
conform
confidence
composition
compound
condescend
coexist
coherence
coincide
communion
communicate
compassion
compromise
component
composer
conceal
compress

LESSON 2 - Practice

1. Study the word list for Unit 29. Understand the meaning of each word.
2. Write each word twice on a separate paper.

LESSON 3 - Spelling Guide

> The prefixes 'co-,' 'com-' and 'con-' mean 'together' or 'with.'

1. Which list words belong to the same family as the words given below?

compose   _____   _____

coexistence   _____

commune   _____   _____

conservation   _____

companion   _____

cooperation   _____

coincidence   _____

competition   _____

conformity   _____

compression   _____

Communication

3. Write all the words in your word list one more time on separate paper.

1. Choose a list word from the group at the left to fit the meanings.

coherence

coincide

condescend

component

compete

compress

a. come down to the same level with something or someone _____

b. press together _____

c. the ability to stick or hold together _____

d. to be in the same position or same time _____

e. an important part of something _____

f. to have a contest with _____

2. Study the syllable divisions of these list words. Learn to spell each syllable. Write the words without syllable divisions.

com-pro-mise _____

co-her-ence _____

com-mu-ni-cate _____

com-pas-sion _____

con-fi-dence _____

con-de-scend _____

com-po-si-tion _____

3. Take your first practice test on all words in the Unit 29 word list.

LESSON 5

Review your word list and take your final test. Write the words in the spaces provided at the back of this book. Ask God for His help with your test.

UNIT 30

WORD BEGINNINGS

LESSON 1 - Vocabulary

Over, In and Under

Circle all list words in these sentences. Spell the list words aloud. Write the sentences on a separate sheet of paper.

1. Your library book is overdue to be returned.

2. We have a midweek prayer service at our church.

3. The fourth graders had a substitute teacher last week.

4. Children must remain in subjection and submission to their parents.

5. We live in a suburban neighborhood near the midwestern city of Chicago.

6. My sister in college is studying for her midterm examinations.

7. We are refunding some of your money because you overpaid your bill.

WORD LIST

overlooked
overpaid
overpower
overshadow
overrated
overruled
overdue
midtown
midterm
midwestern
midnight
midweek
midstream
submarine
subversive
substitute
submission
subjection
substandard
suburban

LESSON 2 - Practice

1. Study the word list for Unit 30. Understand the meaning of each word.
2. Write each word twice on a separate paper.

LESSON 3 - Spelling Guide

> The prefix 'over-' usually means 'above' or 'too much.'
> The prefix 'mid-' means 'in the middle part.'
> The prefix 'sub-' means 'under,' 'below' or 'not quite.'

1. Which list words do these pictures represent? Write the word in the blank under the picture. Write all other list words with the same prefixes.

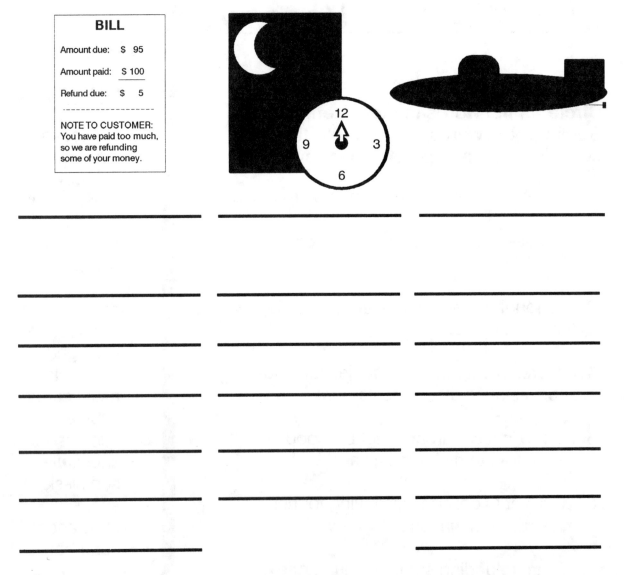

2. Write all the words in your word list one more time on separate paper.

1. WORD ROOTS: Write a list word to fit these descriptions.

| sub = down or under
+
vertere = Latin: to turn |

_____

| sub = down or under
+
missus = Latin: set |

_____

| sub = down or under
+
jectus = Latin: brought |

_____

| sub = down, under, not quite
+
urbs (anus) = Latin: a city |

_____

2. Choose the correct prefix (sub-, over- or mid-) to complete these list words.

_____ruled

_____western

_____standard

_____paid

_____power

_____night

_____stream

_____marine

_____rated

_____term

_____week

_____stitute

_____due

_____shadow

_____versive

_____mission

_____looked

_____town

_____urban

3. Take your first practice test on all words in the Unit 30 word list.

LESSON 5

Review your word list and take your final test. Write the words in the spaces provided at the back of this book. Ask God for His help with your test.

CONTRACTIONS

LESSON 1 - Vocabulary

What's Your Favorite Pet?

Circle all list words in these sentences. Spell the list words aloud. Write the sentences on a separate sheet of paper.

1. My little brother asked for a pet, but my Dad thinks he won't take care of it.

2. Aren't little kittens cute and lovable?

3. Pets are fun to have because they're like good friends.

4. Bob couldn't have a dog because he lived in a small apartment.

5. You're going to enjoy having goldfish because they don't make noise.

6. Horses weren't intended to be house pets.

7. Haven't you fed your parakeet today?

8. I'll always love my dog.

WORD LIST

aren't	he's
won't	she's
can't	what's
isn't	who's
hasn't	that's
don't	you're
weren't	they're
doesn't	we're
haven't	I'm
shouldn't	
couldn't	
wouldn't	
they'll	
you'll	
I'll	
he'll	
she'll	
it'll	
we'll	
it's	
apostrophe	

LESSON 2 - Practice

1. Study the word list for Unit 31. Understand the meaning of each word.
2. Write each word twice on a separate paper.

LESSON 3 - Spelling Guide

> Contractions are abbreviated words (usually formed from a combination of two words) in which an apostrophe (') replaces letters that are left out.

1. Form list words by abbreviating these word phrases into contractions.

should not	_____	will not	_____
are not	_____	could not	_____
they will	_____	she will	_____
it will	_____	that is	_____
they are	_____	it is	_____
she is	_____	you are	_____
would not	_____	has not	_____
will not	_____	he is	_____
cannot	_____	what is	_____
were not	_____	who is	_____
you will	_____	do not	_____
I will	_____		
was not	_____		
have not	_____		
he will	_____		
does not	_____		
is not	_____		

2. Which list word is not a contraction? Write the word.

_____

3. Write all the words in your word list one more time on separate paper.

LESSON 4 - Exercise

1. Circle the letters in these phrases which are left out when forming a contraction. Write the contraction, using an apostrophe to replace the letters you circled.

I am	_____	have not	_____
do not	_____	was not	_____
who is	_____	I will	_____
what is	_____	you will	_____
he is	_____	were not	_____
has not	_____	cannot	_____
you are	_____	will not	_____
it is	_____	would not	_____
that is	_____	she is	_____
he will	_____	they are	_____
she will	_____	it will	_____
could not	_____	they will	_____
we will	_____	are not	_____
is not	_____	should not	_____
does not	_____		

2. Take your first practice test on all words in the Unit 31 word list.

LESSON 5

Review your word list and take your final test. Write the words in the spaces provided at the back of this book. Ask God for His help with your test.

UNIT 32

POSSESSIVES

LESSON 1 - Vocabulary

Belonging

Circle all list words in these sentences. Spell the list words aloud. Write the sentences on a separate sheet of paper.

1. We should work to save America's Christian heritage.

2. Our class's president is David Jones.

3. The Joneses' house is next door to yours.

4. The school children's program is next week.

5. Their parents' pride will be obvious if they do a good job.

6. At Easter time we remember Jesus' death and resurrection.

7. All the churches' pastors in our community held a meeting yesterday.

8. The teachers' meeting will be held today.

WORD LIST

their, theirs
its
your, yours
child's
children's
woman's
women's
class's
classes'
parents'
instructor's
teachers'
library's
government's
churches'
America's
England's
Canada's
Jesus'
Joneses'

LESSON 2 - Practice

1. Study the word list for Unit 32. Understand the meaning of each word.
2. Write each word twice on a separate paper.

LESSON 3 - Spelling Guide

A possessive noun form is used to show that something or someone owns or has (possesses) something. To make a noun show possession:

- add ('s) to a singular noun
- add (') to the name *Jesus* or ancient proper names ending in "-es" such as Moses or Socrates
- add ('s) to a plural noun not ending in "s"
- add (') to a plural noun ending in "s"

Possessive pronouns do not use apostrophes but have their own forms: my, mine, your, yours, his, her, hers, its, our, ours, their, theirs

1. Choose list words to fill the blanks.

a. The books belonging to the library are the _____ books.

b. The song of the class is the _____ song.

c. The age of the child is the _____ age.

d. The laws of the government are the _____ laws.

e. The club to which the women belong is the _____ club.

f. The love of Jesus is _____ love.

g. The queen of England is _____ queen.

h. The directions of the instructor are the _____ directions.

i. The grades given by the teachers are the _____ grades.

j. The picnic for all the children is the _____ picnic.

k. The history of Canada is _____ history.

2. Write all the words in your list one more time on separate paper.

DON'T CONFUSE THESE PRONOUNS

Possessive pronouns: their, theirs. . . Meaning: belongs to them
Contraction: they're. . . . . Meaning: they are

Possessive pronoun: your, yours. . . .Meaning: belongs to you
Contraction: you're. . . . . .Meaning: you are

Possessive pronoun: its. . . . . Meaning: belongs to it
Contraction: it's. . . . . .Meaning: it is

1. Choose: their, theirs or they're

   That is _____ house. The house is _____.

   _____ going on vacation in June.

2. Choose: your, yours or you're

   Where is _____ bicycle? _____ going to be in trouble

   if you left it out in the rain.   The responsibility is _____.

3. Choose: its or it's

   Tell me when _____ nine o'clock.

   You can identify a tree by _____ leaves.

4. Write the possessive form of these words:

   churches_____   parents_____   teachers_____
   library_____   children_____   Joneses_____
   classes_____   women_____   Canada_____

5. Take your first practice test on all words in the Unit 32 word list.

LESSON 5

Review your word list and take your final test. Write the words in the spaces
provided at the back of this book. Ask God for His help with your test.

UNIT 33

IRREGULAR SPELLINGS

LESSON 1 - Vocabulary

Theez R E-Z Werds

Circle all list words in these sentences. Spell the list words aloud. Write the sentences on a separate sheet of paper.

1. Thought for today: "No man is an island."

2. Paul was the apostle to the Gentiles.

3. Getting angry is not the answer.

4. That dress is out of style.

5. The guilty should not go free.

6. When your teacher speaks, you must listen.

7. Go through the gate to enter the castle.

8. Those who live by the sword shall die by the sword.

9. God is the Master Designer of the universe.

WORD LIST

rhyme
guardian
island
apostle
answer
knives
listen
through
thought
though
rough
bough
high
sword
guilty
style
castle
designer
gnome
soften

LESSON 2 - Practice

1. Study the word list for Unit 33. Understand the meaning of each word.
2. Write each word twice on a separate paper.

LESSON 3 - Spelling Guide

> The list words for this unit all have irregular spellings; that is, they are not spelled according to normal rules or phonetic expectations. You must memorize the correct spellings.

1. Correctly spell list words that match these phonetic spellings.

ruff_____   stile_____

gilty_____   cassel_____

bao_____   deeziner_____

sord_____   nome_____

hi_____   sawfen_____

rime_____   nives_____

gardian_____   lissen_____

ieland_____   threw_____

apossel_____   tho_____

anser_____   thawt_____

2. Write all the words in your word list one more time on separate paper.

1. Circle the silent letters in these list words. Write the words.

   knives_____   rhyme_____

   island_____   apostle_____

   sword_____   guardian_____

   castle_____   guilty_____

   soften_____   listen_____

   answer_____   high_____

2. The letter combination 'ough' has five sounds. Write the list word
   in which 'ough' matches the sound given below.

   oo   uff   aw

   _____   _____   _____

             oh   ow (or ao)

        _____   _____

3. Find the word 'gnome' in a dictionary. Write the word in the space
   below left. Write the meaning of the word in the box.

   _____ | _____
                    | _____

4. Take your first practice test on all words in the Unit 33 word list.

LESSON 5

Review your word list and take your final test. Write the words in the spaces
provided at the back of this book. Remember to pray before your test.

UNIT 34

THE CALENDAR

LESSON 1 - Vocabulary

Some Calendar Facts

Circle all list words in these sentences. Spell the list words aloud. Write the sentences on a separate sheet of paper.

1. July is named after Julius Caesar, and August after Augustus, another Roman emperor.

2. The birthstone for April is a diamond.

3. The first day of autumn falls in September.

4. Monday is named after the moon; Saturday is named after the Roman god Saturn.

5. The Roman Emperor Constantine declared Sunday to be the first day of the Christian week.

6. Two great American presidents, George Washington and Abraham Lincoln, were born in February.

7. Thanksgiving Day in the United States falls on the fourth Thursday of November.

WORD LIST

January
February
March
April
May
June
July
August
September
October
November
December
Sunday
Monday
Tuesday
Wednesday
Thursday
Friday
Saturday
calendar

LESSON 2 - Practice

1. Study the word list for Unit 34. Understand the meaning of each word.
2. Write each word twice on a separate paper.

LESSON 3 - Spelling Guide

Names of months and days of the week are usually English forms
of the names of ancient objects of worship: rulers, gods, goddesses,
heavenly bodies. Names of some months are taken from Latin numbers.

1. Can you figure out which month or day name comes from these sources?

Janus, a two-faced Roman god:_____

Julius, a Roman Caesar or emperor:_____

novem, Latin word for nine:_____

Thor's day, for the Germanic/Norse god of thunder:_____

Frigg's day, for the Germanic/Norse goddess of love:_____

septem, Latin word for seven:_____

Mars, the Roman god of war:_____

moon's day:_____   sun's day:_____

Aprilis, another name for Venus, the Roman goddess of love:_____

Augustus, Roman emperor:_____

Tiw's day, for the Germanic god of war:_____

Woden's day, for the chief god of the Germanic people:_____

octo, Latin word for eight:_____

2. Write all the words in your word list one more time on separate paper.

LESSON 4 - Exercise

1. Name the month or day described. Use a dictionary or encyclopedia, if necessary, to help you.

   a. The month in which Christmas is celebrated:_____

   b. The month in which the United States celebrates its independence from England:_____

   c. The day on which most Christians worship together in their churches:_____

   d. The month in which summer begins in the northern hemisphere:_____

   e. The day on which most people begin their school or work week:_____

   f. The day in the exact middle of the week:_____

   g. The month in which spring begins in the northern hemisphere:_____

   h. The month in which Columbus Day is celebrated in America:_____

   i. The eighth month of our Gregorian calendar (the one we use in the western world):_____

   j. The day and month for Thanksgiving Day in the United States:_____ _____

2. Write the list word which is not the name of a day or month:_____

3. Take your first practice test on all words in the Unit 34 word list.

LESSON 5

Review your word list and take your final test. Write the words in the spaces provided at the back of this book. Remember to pray before your test.

MEASURES & ABBREVIATIONS

LESSON 1 - Vocabulary

Circle all list words in these sentences. Spell the list words aloud. Write the sentences on a separate sheet of paper.

1. We live one mile from our church.

2. I bought a gallon of milk, a pound of sugar, and a quart of cream at the store.

3. A postage stamp is about one inch long by three-quarters inch wide.

4. Traveling distance in Europe is measured by the kilometer rather than the mile.

5. Our home is built on an acre of land.

6. Mother gave me a teaspoon of cough syrup when I had a cold.

7. The temperature today is 72 degrees Fahrenheit (22 degrees Celsius).

WORD LIST

gallon - gal.
mile - mi.
quart - qt.
pound - lb.
liter - l.
Fahrenheit - F.
Celsius - C.
centimeter - cm.
kilometer - km.
inch - in.
foot - ft.
cup - c.
teaspoon - tsp. or t.
tablespoon -tbsp. or T.
meter - m.
pint - pt.
ounce - oz.
kilogram - kg.
acre - ac.
ton - tn.

LESSON 2 - Practice

1. Study the word list for Unit 35. Understand the meaning of each word.
2. Write each word twice on a separate paper.

LESSON 3 - Spelling Guide

The terms on the Unit 35 word list all deal with measurements: linear, spatial, volume, or temperature scale. They include words from both the American/British system of measure and the metric system. You must memorize the spellings of the various terms of measurement.

1. Write the list words that these abbreviations stand for.

ft._____
gal._____
F._____
pt._____
mi._____
C._____
c._____
oz._____
qt._____
cm._____
tsp._____
kg._____
lb._____
km._____
tbsp._____
ac._____
l._____
in._____
m._____
tn._____

2. Write the abbreviations of these units of measurement.

liter_____
inch_____
meter_____
ton_____
pound_____
kilometer_____
tablespoon_____
acre_____
quart_____
centimeter_____
teaspoon_____
kilogram_____
mile_____
Celsius_____
cup_____
ounce_____
gallon_____
Fahrenheit_____
foot_____
pint_____

3. Write all the words in your word list one more time on separate paper.

1. Write each of these equations, spelling out in full the abbreviated words.

CONVERSION TABLE

1 in. = 2.5 cm.

1 ft. = 30 cm.

1 yd. = 0.9 m.

1 mi. = 1.6 km.

1 c. = 0.24 l.

1 pt. = 0.47 l.

1 qt. = 0.95 l.

1 gal. = 3.8 l.

1 lb. = 2.2 kg.

2. Take your first practice test on all words in the Unit 35 word list.

LESSON 5

Review your word list and take your final test. Write the words in the spaces provided at the back of this book. Ask God for His help with your test.

UNIT 36

REVIEW

LESSON 1 - Vocabulary

Circle all list words in these sentences. Spell the list words aloud. Write the sentences on a separate sheet of paper.

1. When we go out to eat, I like to order a cheeseburger and french fries.

2. Spilling milk can be carelessness or an accident.

3. My brother thinks he is overworked if he must clean the garage twice a month.

4. You've been a good friend to me.

5. Mr. Arthur takes the subway to work.

6. The countdown has begun for launching the space shuttle.

7. That picture you drew of me is laughable.

8. The rain fell in a constant downpour.

9. The Constitution is the highest law of the land.

WORD LIST

accident
constant
conferee
immovable
laughable
cheeseburger
countdown
foretell
prerecord
coordinate
copilot
constitution
overworked
overdrawn
subdivide
subway
they've
you've
company's
companies'

LESSON 2 - Practice

1. Study the word list for Unit 36. Understand the meaning of each word.
2. Write each word twice on a separate paper.

LESSON 3 - Spelling Guide

> REVIEW - Study all the rules in the Lesson 3 Spelling Guides for Units 25-35. Use some of the rules to complete these exercises.

1. Fill these blanks with list words.

   a. One who confers is a _____.

   b. To tell about something before it happens is to _____.

   c. To record something ahead of time is to_____ it.

   d. That which happens by mistake is an _____.

   e. That which occurs often is _____.

   f. That which is not able to be moved is _____.

   g. If you draw too much out of your bank account, you are _____.

   h. If you are forced to work too much, you are _____.

2. Write the possessive form of these two words:

   company_____ **companies**_____

3. Write contraction forms for these phrases:

   they have_____ **you have**_____

4. Write the two compound words that are on your word list.

   _____   _____

5. Write all the words in your word list one more time on separate paper.

114

1. Choose list words to fit the clues below. Write the words in the boxes. Then read the word in the dark boxes to answer this clue:

It protects our right to speak and worship freely:_____

1. Someone who participates in a conference
2. To record ahead of time
3. Counting backwards to indicate time remaining until an event, such as a rocket launching
4. Underground train
5. To tell the future
6. To work together in a common effort
7. The associate pilot of an aircraft
8. To divide into smaller parts
9. That which is unchanging or faithful
10. An unexpected, undesirable event
11. That which cannot be moved
12. Having taken too much out of a bank account

2. Take your first practice test on all words in the Unit 36 word list.

LESSON 5

Review your word list and take your final test. Write the words in the spaces provided at the back of this book. Ask God for His help with your test.

_____   _____   _____

_____   _____   _____

_____   _____   _____

_____   _____   _____

_____   _____   _____

_____   _____   _____

_____   _____   _____

_____   _____   _____

_____   _____   _____

_____   _____   _____

_____   _____   _____

_____   _____   _____

_____   _____   _____

_____   _____   _____

_____   _____   _____

_____   _____   _____

_____   _____   _____

UNIT 4 TEST	UNIT 5 TEST	UNIT 6 TEST
_____	_____	_____
_____	_____	_____
_____	_____	_____
_____	_____	_____
_____	_____	_____
_____	_____	_____
_____	_____	_____
_____	_____	_____
_____	_____	_____
_____	_____	_____
_____	_____	_____
_____	_____	_____
_____	_____	_____
_____	_____	_____
_____	_____	_____
_____	_____	_____
_____	_____	_____
_____	_____	_____

UNIT 7 TEST	UNIT 8 TEST	UNIT 9 TEST
_____	_____	_____
_____	_____	_____
_____	_____	_____
_____	_____	_____
_____	_____	_____
_____	_____	_____
_____	_____	_____
_____	_____	_____
_____	_____	_____
_____	_____	_____
_____	_____	_____
_____	_____	_____
_____	_____	_____
_____	_____	_____
_____	_____	_____
_____	_____	_____
_____	_____	_____

UNIT 10 TEST

_____

_____

_____

_____

_____

_____

_____

_____

_____

_____

_____

_____

_____

_____

_____

_____

UNIT 11 TEST

_____

_____

_____

_____

_____

_____

_____

_____

_____

_____

_____

_____

_____

_____

_____

_____

UNIT 12 TEST

_____

_____

_____

_____

_____

_____

_____

_____

_____

_____

_____

_____

_____

_____

_____

_____

UNIT 13 TEST

UNIT 14 TEST

UNIT 15 TEST

UNIT 16 TEST

_____
_____
_____
_____
_____
_____
_____
_____
_____
_____
_____
_____
_____
_____
_____
_____
_____
_____

UNIT 17 TEST

_____
_____
_____
_____
_____
_____
_____
_____
_____
_____
_____
_____
_____
_____
_____
_____
_____
_____

UNIT 18 TEST

_____
_____
_____
_____
_____
_____
_____
_____
_____
_____
_____
_____
_____
_____
_____
_____
_____
_____

_____   _____   _____

_____   _____   _____

_____   _____   _____

_____   _____   _____

_____   _____   _____

_____   _____   _____

_____   _____   _____

_____   _____   _____

_____   _____   _____

_____   _____   _____

_____   _____   _____

_____   _____   _____

_____   _____   _____

_____   _____   _____

_____   _____   _____

_____   _____   _____

UNIT 22 TEST

UNIT 23 TEST

UNIT 24 TEST

_____

_____

_____

_____

_____

_____

_____

_____

_____

_____

_____

_____

_____

_____

_____

_____

_____

_____

_____

UNIT 25 TEST

_____

_____

_____

_____

_____

_____

_____

_____

_____

_____

_____

_____

_____

_____

_____

_____

_____

UNIT 26 TEST

_____

_____

_____

_____

_____

_____

_____

_____

_____

_____

_____

_____

_____

_____

_____

_____

_____

UNIT 27 TEST

_____

_____

_____

_____

_____

_____

_____

_____

_____

_____

_____

_____

_____

_____

_____

_____

_____

UNIT 28 TEST

UNIT 29 TEST

UNIT 30 TEST

_____

_____

_____

_____

_____

_____

_____

_____

_____

_____

_____

_____

_____

_____

_____

_____

_____

UNIT 31 TEST

_____

_____

_____

_____

_____

_____

_____

_____

_____

_____

_____

_____

_____

_____

_____

_____

_____

_____

_____

_____

_____

_____

_____

_____

UNIT 32 TEST

_____

_____

_____

_____

_____

_____

_____

_____

_____

_____

_____

_____

_____

_____

_____

_____

_____

UNIT 33 TEST

_____

_____

_____

_____

_____

_____

_____

_____

_____

_____

_____

_____

_____

_____

_____

_____

_____

_____

UNIT 34 TEST

_____
_____
_____
_____
_____
_____
_____
_____
_____
_____
_____
_____
_____
_____
_____
_____
_____

UNIT 35 TEST

_____
_____
_____
_____
_____
_____
_____
_____
_____
_____
_____
_____
_____
_____
_____
_____
_____

UNIT 36 TEST

_____
_____
_____
_____
_____
_____
_____
_____
_____
_____
_____
_____
_____
_____
_____
_____
_____